A WORLD OUTSIDE
The Fiction of Paul Bowles

A WORLD OUTSIDE
The Fiction of Paul Bowles

BY RICHARD F. PATTESON

UNIVERSITY OF TEXAS PRESS
AUSTIN

Publication of this work has been made possible in part by a grant from the Andrew W. Mellon Foundation.

First edition, 1987

Requests for permission to reproduce material from this work should be sent to:
Permissions
University of Texas Press
Box 7819
Austin, Texas 78713-7819

LIBRARY OF CONGRESS CATALOGING-IN-PUBLICATION DATA
Patteson, Richard F. (Richard Francis), 1947–
A world outside.

Bibliography: p.
Includes index.
1. Bowles, Paul, 1910–   —Criticism and interpretation.   I. Title.
PS3552.0874Z78   1987   813'.54   86-19310
ISBN: 978-0-292-79035-3

Frontispiece: Central part of Tangier, Photography Collection, Harry Ransom Humanities Research Center, University of Texas at Austin *to my parents*

Contents

PREFACE   *ix*

ACKNOWLEDGMENTS   *xv*

1. *Interiors and Exteriors (I)*   *1*
2. *Interiors and Exteriors (II)*   *31*
3. *Going Outside*   *54*
4. *The Shapes of Bowles' Fiction*   *84*
5. *Story as Shelter*   *106*

NOTES   *133*

ABBREVIATIONS USED   *141*

BIBLIOGRAPHY   *143*

INDEX   *147*

Preface

PAUL BOWLES is perhaps the most resolutely expatriate American writer since Henry James. He first left the United States in 1929 at the age of eighteen and, after some twenty years of moving about, settled more or less permanently in Tangier, Morocco, where he still resides. During the past five decades Bowles has been a composer, translator, poet, and travel writer, although it is his four novels and more than fifty short stories that have brought him his greatest attention and acclaim. Influences on his writing include Poe, a boyhood enthusiasm; Gertrude Stein, who advised him to give up poetry; Mohammed Mrabet and other Moroccan storytellers whose tales Bowles has recorded and translated over the years; and not least Jane Bowles, whose own fine work was instrumental in turning her husband seriously to the craft of fiction. And there have been many others. But more important than any individual's impact on the development of Bowles' work has been the fact of expatriation itself. Bowles' disinclination to live in (and for the most part, even to write about) the country of his origin—his self-chosen status as an outsider—stamps his art with an indelible mark. Asked why his characters so frequently leave "the safety of a predictable environment" for "an unknown world," Bowles replied, "For one thing there is no 'predictable environment.' Security is a false concept."[1] This question of security, along with the related issues of shelter and exposure, interiority and exteriority, is a concept that animates Bowles' fiction and gives it a distinctive form. It can be tracked unmistakably throughout his writing, from his recollections of earliest childhood in *Without Stopping* to his most complex fictional construct, *The Spider's House*.

Bowles' plots are dominated, as many of his readers have noticed, by journeys out—away from the apparently safe and do-

mestic, toward the dangerous and alien. This is by no means the
only plot structure in Bowles' fiction, but it is the most frequently recurring one, and its traces can be found in all the
others. Bowles has remarked on the similarity between the plots
of *The Sheltering Sky* and "A Distant Episode" as well as between
those of *The Sheltering Sky* and *Up Above the World*. When
asked if Port Moresby, one of the central characters in *The Sheltering Sky*, corresponds to the professor who is the protagonist in
"A Distant Episode," Bowles responded, "They're all the professor. What I mean is that what I wanted to tell was the story of
what the desert can do to us. That was all. The desert is the protagonist."[2] This is precisely what much of Bowles' fiction is
about: coping with a world that is unremittingly *outside*. And
most of Bowles' characters find themselves, to one degree or another, confronting a crisis in which the human need for security
is overwhelmed by the hard metaphysical truth that there is no
interior, no safe place, no humanly made structure that endures.

Bowles' attention to matters of inside and out, belonging and
alienation, closure and openness, originates in the fabric of his
own life and hence helps mark his uniqueness; but that attention
also marks his kinship with other twentieth-century writers
since, in a very broad and general sense, outsidedness and root-
lessness are major strains in modern life and literature. That this
should be true is hardly surprising, considering the history of the
past century, with its breakup of empires, mass migrations, apoca-
lyptic wars, repeated attempts at genocide, and, more recently,
the threat of a thermonuclear end to all things human. These
issues and events have affected the century's artists in myriads of
ways. Bowles himself, like V. S. Naipaul, is one of those writers
on whom the twentieth century has bestowed an uncanny sense
of what it is like never to feel "at home." The political context of
this intense apprehension of dislocation has to do with the re-
alignment of boundaries, the shifting of peoples about the globe,
and the collapse of traditional customs as newly independent
governments rush to modernize. But there is a larger dimension,
too. The long decline of faith throughout the Christian west and
the increasing secularization of life nearly everywhere have contributed to an intuition of exposure and nakedness that transcends politics. And it is this perception of ultimate homelessness

that Paul Bowles, expatriate writer, most powerfully images in his fiction.

The focalizing metaphor that extends throughout Bowles' work and links his autobiographical writings and statements with his fiction is architectural. "If I'm persuaded," he has said, "that our life is predicated upon violence, that the entire structure of what we call civilization, the scaffolding that we've built up over the millennia, can collapse at any moment, then whatever I write is going to be affected by that assumption."[3] Bowles uses the words "structure," "scaffolding," and "built" to talk about civilization because the idea of shelter in his imagination expands from its literal meaning to include social, political, and religious systems as well as other conceptual forms. All of these shelters, from the individual domicile to the complex edifices of society, faith, and personality, are revealed to be extremely delicate and highly susceptible to destruction. Order tends to slip into disorder, calm into violence, form into formlessness, and safe interiors into the vast, unprotected outside. But the effort to fashion shelters goes doggedly on in Bowles. His characters are nothing if not persistent in their determination to make a strange, nonhuman world seem more like home, and their project, though never entirely successful, invests them with a dignity sometimes approaching heroism.

There has been surprisingly little critical treatment of Bowles' work. A recent issue of *The Review of Contemporary Fiction*, in fact, roughly doubled the number of Bowles articles in print. Only three book-length studies of Bowles have been undertaken, to my knowledge: Lawrence D. Stewart's *Paul Bowles: The Illumination of North Africa;* Johannes Bertens' *The Fiction of Paul Bowles: The Soul Is the Weariest Part of the Body;* and Wayne Pounds' *Paul Bowles: The Inner Geography.* All three of these books, each different in its emphasis, deserve notice for their thoughtful, serious consideration of Bowles' canon. Stewart discusses the three novels and many of the stories that take place in North Africa, as well as "Pages from Cold Point," which does not. He more than adequately chronicles Bowles' travels in that region and provides a great deal of other biographical information. Stewart seems particularly interested in the circumstances surrounding the composition of various works, but he also goes into much interpretive detail. His last chapter is dominated by a consideration of Bowles' most recent stories to date (1974) and his translations. Bertens' study treats Bowles' fiction as portraying the spiritual malaise of westerners and their largely futile attempts to alleviate it. For Bertens, love and companionship offer the only means of effectively escaping from (or at least of mitigating) the nihilism brought about by the failure of rationalism and the concomitant ascendancy of mass society.

Like Bertens, Pounds discusses Bowles' work as a critique of western civilization, but Pounds, drawing on both Freud and R. D. Laing, goes into much greater depth in his analysis of Bowles' "anatomy of the disease of our time and place." Seeing Bowles' work as "part of the larger development through which American literature has sought to assimilate the experience of the frontier," Pounds argues that the quest of the typical Bowles protagonist is a psychological one: "The Western pilgrim is driven to encounter primitive landscapes, primitive peoples, or the primitive within his own self, but the basic quest is for self-destruction." The "civilized ego," which has become "constricting and brittle," journeys through "psychic landscapes," drawn toward a knowledge that will bring about its annihilation.[4] Although Pounds' analysis of this aspect of Bowles' fiction contains many valuable insights and points out a number of interesting connections between Bowles and earlier American writers, particularly Poe, it seems to me to rely too heavily on the "psychic structure" described by Laing in *The Divided Self*. Despite his protestations to the contrary, Pounds' study tends somewhat toward the Procrustean bed. Nevertheless, his emphasis on the self-destructive impulse is important, because it highlights a feature that many readers notice in Bowles' fiction: the apparent allure of danger and the possibility of annihilation. It is undeniable that many Bowles characters feel compelled to place their very existence in jeopardy, and that they experience a kind of exhilaration in doing so; but I will attempt to demonstrate that they expose themselves in this way not so much from a desire for self-destruction as, paradoxically, from a longing for self-preservation. The purpose is not always fully articulate in their own minds, but they invariably trend, or drift, outward to chal-

lenge the dominance of the outside world—not to surrender
to it.

The book that follows first takes up the forming of Bowles' fiction through architectural concepts and the various lineaments,
both formal and thematic, that those concepts assume. I begin
with a discussion of one of his most vivid and personal articula-
tions of the architectural metaphor—a frightening childhood
memory recounted in *Without Stopping*—and go on, in Chapters 1 and 2, to pursue the widening circle of meanings (psychological, sociological, philosophical) that this brief narrative generates. Chapter 3 places Bowles in the tradition of other writers,
particularly Haggard and Conrad, who have dealt with the domestication of the alien "outside" in terms of cultural contact
and conflict. Chapter 4 moves to matters of construction and
technique and leads into Chapter 5, where I explore the sheltering function of storytelling itself in Bowles' work. I should add a
final note on my method. It is exceedingly difficult to write about
the fiction of a man who has created so many narratives, both
long and short. I have chosen not to organize this book in a conventional way, with a chapter devoted to each novel and a chapter or two to the stories. Indeed, it is arguable that there is not
a really exhaustive exegesis of any single Bowles work in these
pages. Instead of a reader's guide I offer a way of reading Bowles.
Such an approach necessarily entails the omission or slighting of
certain stories; it also entails, largely because of the coherence of
Bowles' vision and the resulting recurrence of themes and patterns, some repetition, some circling back over familiar territory
in search of the truest configurations in Bowles' art.

It must be obvious from my references to autobiography and
interviews that this study does not, in the manner recently fash-
ionable, treat intention as irrelevant or the author as nonexistent.
My approach does presuppose a connection between the human
being and the stories he tells through his writings. Nevertheless,
I do not mean to use autobiography as a "key" to "unlock" se-
crets within fictional texts. No biographical material will be
found here except that which bears the authority of Paul Bowles'
own articulation. While there may well be much valuable information about Bowles' life (particularly his personal life) that can

be researched and brought to bear on his fiction, those endeavors will have to await a biographical critic or critical biographer. I do believe, however, that the factual "stories" a writer consciously chooses to tell about himself are a vital part of his imaginative legacy and can be scrutinized as usefully as can any of his other writings. It is not my purpose to confer on autobiography, interviews, and other nonfictional texts a privileged status, but neither will I ignore them or deny them their own validity. There are conceptual insignia within these utterances that can be traced throughout Bowles' creative work and that compellingly shape his fiction.

Acknowledgments

I WOULD LIKE to thank, first of all, Paul Bowles for his unfailing courtesy and cooperation during my visits to him in 1984 and 1986.

I would further like to thank the staff of the Harry Ransom Humanities Research Center at the University of Texas; Dave Oliphant and Tom Zigal, editors of *The Library Chronicle;* and the staff at the University of Texas Press.

I am indebted also to Tammy Dickerson, for her patient and efficient typing; Anthony Foster, for his proofreading skill and steady friendship; my students, for their help in developing ideas as my own thinking about Bowles evolved in the classroom; and especially my mother and father for all their encouragement over the years.

Mississippi State University has been the source of much moral and still more financial support, making possible essential trips to both Austin, Texas, and Tangier, Morocco. Special thanks are due to Joseph E. Milosh, Jr., and to the English Department's Travel Committee, to Dean Edward L. McGlone of the College of Arts and Sciences, to Vice Presidents Marion T. Loftin and Ralph E. Powe of the Office of Graduate Studies and Research, to Dean Lewis R. Brown and the Academic Excellence Committee, and to Charles Lowery and the Institute for the Humanities. Additional financial assistance was provided by a Travel to Collections Grant from the National Endowment for the Humanities.

The friends who have contributed in oblique yet important ways to the completion of this book are too numerous to acknowledge individually, but two of them can hardly be omitted: Don Graham, who first told me to read Paul Bowles, and Tom Sauret, who first urged me to write about him.

R.F.P.

A WORLD OUTSIDE
The Fiction of Paul Bowles

1. *Interiors and Exteriors (I)*

PAUL BOWLES' EXPATRIATION began, in his own mind, shortly after he was born. Never quite comfortable at home, he endured a rather solitary childhood made more difficult by his father's constant criticism. "His mere presence meant misery,"[1] Bowles recalls in his autobiography, *Without Stopping*. Getting away, whether to the homes of various relatives, to the public library, or simply to the privacy of his own room, became one of his most pressing objectives. Bowles describes in *Without Stopping* instance after instance of his father's hostility and even brutality toward him, but nowhere does he more bluntly frame the experience in terms of primal terror than in his reconstruction of a story told to him by his maternal grandmother:

> "Your father wanted to kill you. . . . When you were only six weeks old, he did it. He came home one terrible night when the wind was roaring and the snow was coming down—a real blizzard—and marched straight into your room, opened the window up wide, walked over to your crib and yanked you out from under your warm blankets, stripped you naked, and carried you over to the window where the snow was sailing in. And that devil just left you there in a wicker basket on the windowsill for the snow to fall on." (*WS* 38–39)

This incident, which Bowles remembers as "only too possible" (*WS* 38), may or may not actually have occurred. What is important to the mapping of Bowles' imagination is the mental imprint the story made on him—an impression strong enough for him to write it down years later in these words and to give it a prominent position in a book that purports to be a factual account of his life.

Later, when Bowles was twelve, something happened that seems, at least in his retelling of it, to recapitulate some of the outlines of his grandmother's story. The family home had been burglarized while everyone was away for the weekend. The event had an effect on Bowles that came back to haunt him:

> . . . one night I had a dream, and I dreamed that I was standing downstairs in the dining room, looking toward the windows. I went over and pulled back the first curtains, and the second curtains, and saw that one of the windows had been broken and was open and the screen outside cut and unhooked. . . . But even as I looked at the curtains, I saw part of a hand slip between them. Then the lights went out, I was being strangled, and that awakened me. (*WS* 55)

The next morning Bowles discovered that the window had indeed been "broken and the screening cut . . . and in precisely the same places" (*WS* 56) as in his dream. This strange event "temporarily shook" Bowles' faith "in a rationally motivated cosmos" (*WS* 56). His faith in a rational cosmos was to be shaken further as the years passed, but the significance of this particular experience should not be underestimated. Bowles' dream shares with the story told him by his grandmother an implicit model of human experience: an interior presumed to be secure, and an exterior known to be hostile; a safe, humanized haven of rationality surrounded by an irrational, threatening cosmos (or more accurately, chaos). In both versions, the "safe" interior is violated by the world outside. If the earlier version is more frightful, it is only because the potential source of danger, the father, is normally and complacently thought to be part of the safe, protective inside.

Tzvetan Todorov, in an analysis of Henry James' fiction, posits the existence of "that general plan which governs all the rest, as it appears in each of his works." Drawing on James' own terminology, Todorov calls this plan the figure in the writer's carpet. "We may assume," he continues, "that an author comes closer in some works than in others to that 'figure in the carpet' which epitomizes and sustains the totality of his writings."[2] The open window, the exposed, vulnerable individual, and the encroachment of a cold outside on a not very safe interior together constitute something like a figure in Paul Bowles' carpet. While it may be argued that what Todorov means by "figure" lies exclusively in the literary texts themselves and Bowles' seems to have its origin in the author's life, it will become evident that Bowles' own imaginative watermark, although clearly generated out of authorial experience, is explicitly immanent in the texts as well. The diction in the grandmother's story from *Without Stopping* is almost excessive in its emphasis: terrible night, roaring wind, snow coming down, blizzard, opened window, stripped naked, window, snow, windowsill, snow. Yet the images formed from these words not only reappear in but, to redirect Todorov's expression somewhat, epitomize and sustain the totality of Bowles' fiction. It may be worth noting also that the words *expatriation* and *father* have the same Indo-European root. Bowles' sense of exile and his conviction that "security is a false concept" have a much deeper explanatory source than the mere fact of living abroad.

Although a catalogue of open windows and raging weather in Bowles' fiction would fill many pages, only a few examples are necessary to suggest the pervasiveness and importance of this "figure." The plot of *Up Above the World,* for instance, turns sharply on the opening of a window. Early in that novel a woman with the rather obvious name of "Mrs. Rainmantle" refuses to sleep in a hotel room because the door does not lock. She switches to a presumably more secure room but is murdered during the night by a man (in the employ of her own son) who climbs in through the window. That which lies outside is presented as potentially hostile and threatening, yet the barriers, the shelters, erected to keep the danger out are insufficient. This pattern persists in all of Bowles' work. *The Spider's House* is rich with references to open and broken windows as well as to bombs, gunfire, and riots just outside those windows. In "Midnight Mass," one of Bowles' later stories, a broken window presages the house's further deterioration and the owner's eventual expulsion from it. "How Many Midnights" records the panic that sets in when a young woman's life falls apart. As the woman waits in a New York apartment for a fiancé who never arrives, the conception she has of her life as an orderly, manageable construct gradually disintegrates. By the end of the story, her opening of a window to let the winter wind blow through signals an unspoken acknowledgment that her sense of security cannot withstand violation from the world outside.

A commonly recurring motif in Bowles' fiction is the individual exposed to the external world. The vulnerable figure is frequently a child, but even the adult protagonists are so stripped of defenses that they bear the unmistakable imaginative imprint of the baby on the windowsill. "The Delicate Prey," one of Bowles' finest stories, is also one of the purest fictional realizations of that imprint. The story begins with the decision of a family of leather merchants to leave their home in Tabelbala (in present-day Algeria) and go to Tessalit, far to the south (in present-day Mali). The party consists of two older brothers and their young nephew, Driss. The journey is a dangerous one because, if they take the faster, westernmost route, they will have to pass through a region "contiguous to the lands of the plundering Reguibat tribes,"[3] who are known for their savagery. The merchants are Filala—that is, their family originates in the Tafilalet area of southeastern Morocco. During the course of the journey they encounter a man who at first is feared to be a Reguiba but turns out to be a friendly and civilized Moungari. They agree to travel together as far as Taoudeni, a town midway between Tabelbala and Tessalit, deep in the Sahara. What follows is extraordinarily gruesome and is largely responsible for earning Paul Bowles an undeserved reputation as a "gothic" writer.[4] The Moungari lures the two uncles out of Driss' sight on the pretext of shooting gazelles, the "delicate prey" of the story's title. He instead shoots the two men and then, driven wild by hashish, shoots Driss in the arm, severs his penis with a knife, cuts an incision into his abdomen, and stuffs the dismembered organ into it. Afterward he sodomizes the boy, leaves him to suffer alive all night, and finally slits his throat. Somewhat later when Filala friends of the family travel to Tessalit, they discover the Moungari's crime and are permitted by the French authorities to deal with him as they see fit. They take him to a remote area of the desert and bury him in a pit, leaving him to die slowly with only his head above ground.

Bowles has been criticized for injecting violence and brutality into his fiction for shock value alone,[5] but the horror, though admittedly sometimes shocking, is seldom gratuitous. Here in "The Delicate Prey" it is essential to Bowles' creative purpose, which is to find an intelligible dramatic form for an outsidedness so absolute as to be quite beyond ordinary human comprehension. From the very beginning of the story it is clear that the exposure pattern will dominate. The journey is to be a movement from the familiar to the unfamiliar, from a comfortable "inside" to an unknown and potentially hazardous outside. Conflicting signals in the first few paragraphs make the danger seem real and at the same time lead the reader to expect that the enterprise might still succeed. The Reguibat do pose a threat, but they have not attacked a caravan for "a long time" and they are thought to have "lost the greater part of their arms and ammunition, and, more important still, their spirit" (*CS* 165). Moreover, such a small band as Driss and his uncles would not present much of a temptation to the Reguibat, who are "traditionally rich with loot from all Rio de Oro and Mauretania" (*CS* 165). They set out "toward the bright horizon" (*CS* 165), feeling relatively confident. The fact that they meet their destruction not at the hands of the Reguibat but at those of a Moungari universalizes the danger. It is simply "out there," unidentifiable and therefore impossible to avoid.

Shelter is ineffectual in "The Delicate Prey." All those structures—family, society, religion, art—that keep us what we loosely call civilized prove to be vulnerable. Driss has in his uncles not one but two father figures, yet the protective, nurturing function of the family is nullified by their abrupt murders. Nor does religion seem to matter. Although the uncles "engage in complicated theological discussions" (*CS* 165), their theology can neither prevent nor adequately account for their arbitrary deaths. As if to accentuate this point, the narrator discloses that the Filala trust the Moungari because "Moungar is a holy place in that part of the world, and its few residents are treated with respect by the pilgrims who go to visit the ruined shrines nearby" (*CS* 166). The ritual of making tea "to seal their friendship" (*CS* 166) becomes a cruel mockery. Late in the story when the Filala friends capture the Moungari, he is again brewing tea. They tie him up and contemptuously, without sharing or asking permission, drink what he has made. This ceremony, an important social structure in the Islamic world, is stripped of its essentially protective significance.

One of the human-created structures most insistently hinted at in the story is art. Driss plays songs on his flute during the journey. One of the uncles wanders off toward the Moungari (and to his death) "singing a song from Tafilalet" (CS 168). That the song's origin is the family's ancestral home—the place where a Filali should feel safest—underscores the grim irony of the shooting that immediately follows. A bit later, after killing both brothers, the Moungari himself sings. And he sings again at the story's end: "When they had gone the Moungari fell silent, to wait through the cold hours for the sun that would bring first warmth, then heat, thirst, fire, visions. The next night he did not know where he was, did not feel the cold. The wind blew dust along the ground into his mouth as he sang" (CS 172). The stories we tell ourselves, the songs we sing to calm our fears, seem to change very little in the long run. Bowles has said that in tales like this one the desert (his most vivid figure for the world outside) is the main character. And in fact it is hard not to be struck by the way in which the story's last song concludes, with the intransigently alien earth blowing into the Moungari's mouth, robbing him at last of his song and his humanity.

The stilling of the artistic voice in "The Delicate Prey" (every character who sings dies brutally) is subtly interwoven with the thwarting of sexual creativity. The boy's "sex that sprouted" is cut off "with the motion of a reaper wielding a sickle" (CS 170). The implantation of the severed penis in the incision is a bizarre parody of a normal sexual act, a kind of coition that can lead only to death. The similar implantation of the Moungari's body in the earth and the earth's subsequent entry into his singing mouth make almost explicit the connection between procreative and artistic impulses. One is to make life; the other, to sustain it. And both are stopped in Bowles' story. At one point the narrator observes, referring to the Moungari's hashish-induced delirium, that "a man can escape very far from the world of meaning" (CS 169). Indeed, the world of meaning is finally impossible *not* to escape, whether one wishes to or not. The fact that the self and the creations of the self can be so easily and so arbitrarily extinguished is the definitive implication of the outsidedness experienced by Bowles' characters.

There are many variations of the child in the opened window in Bowles' work. Many of these exposed persons are actually adults, like Port Moresby in *The Sheltering Sky,* who dies of typhoid in a remote desert town, or the Slades in *Up Above the World,* who are drugged and murdered by the same psychotic who has had his mother killed. But many of them are children in fact. Of these perhaps the most common is the neglected child, the waif who is left to make his own way in a hostile world. In "Señor Ong and Señor Ha" a boy named Nicho, who lives with his aunt in a Mexican village, befriends Luz, an albino girl whose "parents were having quarrels at home" (*CS* 177). Their friendship endures, and with each other's company they manage to craft a kind of emotional interior for themselves, but the price of their fragile sense of security is Nicho's increasing involvement in the drug trafficking of his aunt's Chinese lover. The story's final impression, focusing on the child's corruption, is not one of comfort or assurance. "Reminders of Bouselham," a more recent story, is interesting in that it contains a double displacement. The narrator lives with his mother, but in a situation reminiscent of Flannery O'Connor's "The Comforts of Home" and "The Lame Shall Enter First," he is gradually supplanted by an outsider—in this case Bouselham, the Moroccan boy his mother has taken for a lover:

> There is no doubt that Mother changed in certain respects during the time Bouselham was living in the house. She did buy a secondhand Porsche convertible for him, and this was certainly most unlike her. Her manner became distant; she seemed uninvolved in all the things that heretofore had been her life. When I suggested that I move out of the house and take a flat in town, she merely raised her eyebrows. (*CS* 388)

But Bouselham, too, eventually loses his place: "His dismissal had been summary, with no explanation offered." The narrator remarks that "her arbitrary behavior had bewildered and aggrieved him. The way he saw it, he had been turned out of the house for no reason at all" (*CS* 391–392). Although there are "reasons" implicit in the story for both rejections (the son's and Bouselham's), they are unconvincing to the characters who are rejected. The story ends with the house sold and the mother gone off to Italy.

Sometimes the neglect/desertion pattern escalates into overt violence, and these are the most painful of Bowles' tales to read, the ones closest to nightmare. In "Doña Faustina," the most ghastly of all, a Mexican woman murders children, eats their hearts, and feeds their remains to a giant crocodile she keeps in a tank in her garden. "If I Should Open My Mouth" is one of Bowles' few stories set in the United States and one of his few narrated in the first person. Its narrator, who records his thoughts in the form of a journal, gradually reveals himself to be a man with a tenuous hold on sanity. All that keeps his mind together is a plot to replace packages of chewing gum with poisoned ones in vending machines in the New York subway system. For days he is bewildered by the newspapers' curious silence about the deaths that must have occurred, until at last he discovers the contaminated packages in a bureau drawer. He has only imagined that he made the substitutions. All during this time he has been increasingly annoyed by the next-door neighbors' little girl, Dorothy, whom he, a malevolent Wizard of Oz, characterizes as "a horror" (CS 258). At the end of the story, just after angrily pushing Dorothy's tricycle down the front steps and into the street, he decides what to do with the poisoned gum: "After dinner I am going to take all forty boxes to the woods behind the school and throw them onto the rubbish heap there. . . . Let the kids have them" (CS 259). As the narrator slips rapidly into a world of paranoid delusion, it becomes evident that he is as defenseless as the "kids" who may die (if the entire plot is not a delusion). "It's too childish a game to go on playing at my age" (CS 259), he admits, revealing that he, too, although in one sense the aggressive adult, is in another sense the child in the window.

Bowles returns again and again to the adult/child relationship, but nowhere more cogently than in "Pages from Cold Point," "The Frozen Fields," and "Kitty." These are the stories—from the early, middle, and later stages of his career—that most conspicuously display the figure in Bowles' carpet. In "Pages from Cold Point" the protective function of the family structure is considerably undermined. The story begins with the narrator's decision, after the death of his wife, Hope, to give up his college teaching job and move with his teen-aged son, Racky, to a remote island in the West Indies. The son proves to be aggressively and promiscuously homosexual. Eventually his preying upon the

men and boys of the island forces his father to set him up in a
Havana apartment where he can do what he pleases without getting into trouble. But the story's real drama unfolds as Norton,
the father, gradually and only half intentionally reveals his own
desire for the boy.

The disclosures begin almost immediately. Norton, after ex-
pressing his loathing for his elder brother, Charles, reports a conversation that occurs just before his departure for the islands. In
a rapid series of exchanges Charles says to him, "By God, if I
could stop you legally, I would!" and "You're not fit to have
custody of the kid" and "D'ye think I've forgotten?" and finally,
"Get wise to yourself! You're not fooling anybody, you know"
(CS 84). The reader naturally wonders why Charles wants to
stop Norton, why he thinks his brother is "not fit to have custody," and what, exactly, he has not forgotten. The only explanation given overtly by Norton is that Charles is stupid. A few
paragraphs later, however, new clues emerge with Norton's references to Racky's "angelic face" (CS 85), his "lithe body . . .
smooth skin . . . animal energy and grace" (CS 87). Some of his
observations appropriate outright the language of romantic love:

> . . . God knows I can never even think of the boy without that famil-
> iar overwhelming sensation of delight and gratitude for being vouch-
> safed the privilege of sharing my life with him. What he takes so
> completely as a matter of course, our daily life here together, is a
> source of never-ending wonder to me; and I reflect upon it a good
> part of each day, just sitting here being conscious of my great good
> fortune in having him all to myself, beyond the reach of prying eyes
> and malicious tongues. (CS 86)

Once again Norton's choice of words stirs the reader's suspicions.
What might "prying eyes" see or "malicious tongues" tell? And
again Charles is blamed. What does he know that the reader
must guess?

When an official from the local constabulary informs Norton
of Racky's indiscretions, Norton reflects, "It was as if I wanted to
believe it" (CS 94). The consummation of the story, and evidently
of the father/son relationship as well, occurs shortly afterward
when Norton finds Racky naked in his (Norton's) bed and joins
him there. An offhand remark by Racky a few days later confirms

that this arrangement has continued. Although Norton takes Racky to Havana and himself returns to live alone at Cold Point, it is plain that for a brief time father and son have engaged in a sexual relationship—certainly in fantasy and probably in fact. Lawrence Stewart, in a perceptive and persuasive analysis, argues that the secret to which Charles alludes during his heated exchange with Norton is nothing less than a homosexual affair that took place when the brothers were young. Norton does seem to admit that *something* happened between them years earlier: "The effect he [Charles] has on me dates from an early period in our lives, from days I dislike to recall" (*CS* 85). Racky appears to have overheard part of the conversation between Charles and Norton. If so, he has heard Charles say, "But just remember, I've got your number all right, and if there's any trouble with the boy I'll know who's to blame" (*CS* 84–85). Stewart concludes from all this that when Racky subsequently slips into his father's bed, and a few days later suggests that they invite Charles over to visit them at Cold Point, he is engaging in subtle blackmail. The result is what Racky wants: freedom to pursue his inclinations in a distant place, unencumbered by interference by his father or anyone else. Norton eventually sacrifices the companionship of his son in order to prevent an even greater interruption of the "nothingness" he cultivates.[6]

Despite his frequent ruminating about the joys of doing nothing in the face of civilization's probable self-annihilation in the near future, Norton's relationship to Racky—not his philosophy—is the dramatic center of "Pages from Cold Point." The story's most striking image, and the point at which what I have called Bowles' watermark most clearly shows through, is the figure of Norton standing over his naked son while the son sleeps. This scene obliquely recalls the moment in "The Delicate Prey" when the Moungari rips off Driss' clothing and rapes him. Both tableaux place an older man above the helpless and exposed body of a boy child. It is the baby in the windowsill once more. But it must be remembered that in this story the "victim," Racky, is also a predator, and that his father is among *his* delicate prey. Racky's newly acquired propensity for taking off his clothes in front of Norton makes clear that the exploitation works both ways. Norton fulfills his parental role only perfunctorily, and always in his own self-interest. When that interest dictates that he send Racky out on his own, he does so immediately, with little regard for the boy's youth. But if Racky lacks the security of a truly nurturing father, Norton's own shelter—the dreamlike idyll with his son—also collapses. As Stewart points out (*PB* 47), an early draft in the Humanities Research Center reveals that Racky's original name was "Rocky" and the story's original title was "The Sheltering Rocks."[7]

"Pages from Cold Point" is a disturbing and profoundly sad account of a father and son who expose each other to an awful truth. Even within a familiar and presumably safe construct (here the family itself), one can still be outside. "The Frozen Fields" brings the outside in still more directly, and again the dramatic nexus is tension between a father and a son. The story is ostentatiously about fathers, windows, and snow, and it doubles back more sharply than anything else in Bowles' fiction to the "self-selected memory"[8] of himself as a baby stripped and exposed to the elements. It is also, Bowles has told me, consciously autobiographical.[9] The story takes place during a Christmas holiday visit by a boy and his parents to the rural home of the mother's family, and in the very first scene, on the train, the differences between inside and outside, safety and danger, are brought to the foreground. The boy, Donald, tries to scratch pictures on the icy windowpane, but his father roughly stops him, making him angry and resentful. Soon afterward Donald reflects on the possibility that there may be wolves in the woods. The beginning of the story, then, sets up an inside (safety)/outside (danger) equation while hinting, through the father's hostility, that the formula may be less simple than that.

During the summers spent on his grandparents' farm, Donald has felt comfortable and secure, but now he observes that the land has "lost its intimacy, become bare and unprotected" (*CS* 263). The change has less to do with the blanket of snow than with the oppressive presence of his father. As in "Pages from Cold Point," the story's main conflict is related to the question of sexual identity. Donald is not quite seven years old, but already his father is concerned about his strength and manliness. He wants his son to be disciplined and tough, as he conceives himself to be. For his part Donald regards his father, who is brutal and domineering with everyone, and whom no one really likes, as "a grave danger" (*CS* 262). Yet to his father's displeasure he is not at all put off by his apparently homosexual Uncle Ivor[10] or by Ivor's effeminate friend Mr. Gordon, who later remarks that Donald reminds him of himself when he was that age. During a row at the dinner table, when Donald's father becomes quite abusive on the subject of Uncle Ivor, Donald is struck not so much by any "oddness" on Ivor's part as by his father's frightening display of temper. Just after dinner, in fact, he takes advantage of Uncle Ivor's invitation to go with him to the henhouse, thereby precipitating his father's second and more significant outburst. Uncle Ivor has said gently to the boy, "Come on in and shut the door. You'll let all the heat out," but Donald's father, truly a part of the chill outside, flings open the door and roars a command that echoes from the remotest depths of Paul Bowles' childhood: "Come out here!" (*CS* 273). The nature of the father's disappointment with his son immediately becomes apparent. Almost instantly he starts to badger the boy, then dares him to hit a tree with a snowball. Thinking again of the wolves that might be aroused by such an act, Donald refuses. His father takes the refusal as a sign of weakness as well as of disobedience:

> Before Donald knew what was happening, his father had seized him with one hand while he bent over and with the other scooped up as much snow as he could. . . . Suddenly he was rubbing the snow violently over Donald's face, and at the same time that Donald gasped and squirmed, he pushed what was left of it down his neck. As he felt the wet, icy mass sliding down his back, he doubled over. His eyes were squeezed shut; he was certain his father was trying to kill him. (*CS* 274)

This is a vivid fictional re-enactment of the scene recalled in *Without Stopping*—transformed and mitigated by art from attempted murder to an assault that merely seems like attempted murder.

Both "Pages from Cold Point" and "The Frozen Fields" are to some degree fictional projections of a desire for revenge against the male parent. In "Pages from Cold Point" the element of revenge is cloaked by the character's obvious affection for his father, perversely directed though it may be. Racky flirts with and probably seduces Norton, but he does not appear to do so out of a conscious desire to punish him. "The Frozen Fields" brings the child's anger and longing for vengeance to the very surface of the narrative. Early in the story Donald fantasizes that a wolf will come raging out of the woods, smash through the dining room window, seize his father by the throat, and be "gone again with his prey still between his jaws" (*CS* 266). And at the end, after his mother tucks him in bed, he lies awake "listening to the sound of the fine snow as the wind drove it against the panes" (*CS* 276). He imagines that the wolf is out there and that they are friends: "Then he lay down beside him, putting his heavy head in Donald's lap. Donald leaned over and buried his face in the shaggy fur of his scruff" (*CS* 276). Donald has successfully, at least for the time being, domesticated the outside, bringing it into a new interior of his own creation. And a denizen of that formerly outside world, the wolf, becomes the agent of destruction of the father, who is the real source of Donald's discomfort. If the story is read as a gloss on the autobiographical recollection (instead of the other way around), the wolf's crashing through the window can be seen as a rather fine instance of poetic justice. In reflecting on his own past, Bowles once remarked, "Even as a small child, I was always trying to get away." [11] "The Frozen Fields" ends with the image of Donald and the wolf together, running off across the fields, faster and faster—one might even say, without stopping.

"Kitty," a much later and somewhat gentler treatment of parents, children, and the need for security, is couched as a hypothesis of total safety from a child's point of view. The story is one of Bowles' several tales of transference. The title character undergoes a startling transformation from little girl to kitten. Whether the change is just in her mind or actually occurs "in fact" is not made clear and is finally not very important. Her attitude toward the change is important, however. When it first begins her mother is not interested—she has "no time for such things." [12] As the whiskers and fur continue to grow (or not to grow), her mother continues not to notice; nor, for that matter, do the neighbors. Kitty feels increasingly snug in her feline world, and she feels increasingly that other people are outside it. The structure that she builds for herself is not unlike that of Donald in

"The Frozen Fields." But isolation is not at all what Kitty wants. What *she* desires most is a secure interior that includes her family.

When the transformation is complete, Kitty tears off her nightgown and wanders over to a neighbor's house. At this point Mrs. Tinsley, the neighbor, recognizes her as a kitten and tries to keep her in the cellar, but this is "not at all what Kitty wanted" (*MM* 109). When she escapes and returns home, she finds her mother crying over the torn nightgown, but her parents still neglect (or fail to recognize) her: "No one paid the slightest attention to Kitty" (*MM* 110). Kitty goes back to the Tinsleys', but she continues to return frequently to her own house. In the story's most resonant scene, she peers wistfully at her father through the familiar Bowles window:

> She would go to her house at night and look in through the window to see her father sitting alone reading the paper. This was how she knew that her mother had gone away. Even if she cried and pushed her claws against the window, her father paid no attention to her, and she knew that he would never let her in. Only her mother would do that. (*MM* 110)

When her mother comes home (apparently from a long stay in a hospital), she does exactly that, and Kitty is happy at last, assured that her mother loves her "and that her father would learn to love her" (*MM* 111). Nowhere in his fiction does Bowles come closer to portraying a loving, comfortable relationship between parents and a child, and even here he can do so only by imagining the child as a pet. In response to a remark that his characters are "asocial," Bowles retorted, "Are they? Or are they merely outside and wishing they were inside?"[13] The poignancy and force of Bowles' writing derives from his own intimate knowledge of the situation in which his characters so frequently find themselves: wishing to be inside, with the window safely closed.

The concept of a safe enclosure threatened by a dangerous, unknown exterior associated with unreason and oblivion is not an idea that Paul Bowles invented. The inside/outside dichotomy is as old as the first fire around which men and women gathered for comfort and a fleeting sense of protection from the vast darkness. Nevertheless, that concept has not often been put to such thoroughgoing artistic use, nor has it often grown so obviously out of an artist's experience and memories. Anxiety is the ruling passion in Bowles' fictional universe. He understands, and his characters sometimes intuit, that, in Wilhelm Worringer's words, "the urge to abstraction is the outcome of a great inner unrest inspired in man by the phenomena of the outside world."[14] Or as Philip Stevick puts it, "The impulse to enclose . . . is a basic property of the mind."[15] It is a property that originates in anxiety about the stability of the self and of the universe. Many people undoubtedly take order and meaning for granted. Others, like Joseph Conrad, Paul Bowles, and Thomas Pynchon, know that "the city is only the desert in disguise."[16] Bowles, although he dislikes Pynchon's work, would agree with him in this one respect: the function of architectural form, and of form itself, is to humanize the nonhuman, to make the great outside seem bearable, the mysterious intelligible, and to create the semblance of a home for human beings where none can really exist.[17]

The psychological roots of this project have been explored by Gaston Bachelard, who argues that our notion of "home" is primal. A state of well-being *precedes* the experience of being "cast into the world,"[18] but with consciousness comes knowledge of that expulsion, and a concomitant state of anxiety and alienation. We can "return," briefly, to a sense of serenity that is "prehuman" (*PS* 10), but only through dreams and daydreams. Bachelard notes that "many children draw a house spontaneously while dreaming over their paper and pencil" (*PS* 72) and calls the house image "a veritable principle of psychological integration" (*PS* xxxii). He convincingly postulates the human need to come back to an imaginative sense of the primal house, but he also insists on the house's fragility: "A nest—and this we *understand* right away—is a precarious thing, and yet it sets us to *daydreaming of security*" (*PS* 102). Those daydreams and that security are fragile, too. When we dream, "we relive the instinct of the bird" (*PS* 103), but because we are rational, conscious human beings, we know that the nest is not really safe. Bachelard refers to "the illusion of protection" (*PS* 5), and he suggests that the primal house must be repeatedly rebuilt: "A house constitutes a body of images that give mankind proofs or illusions of sta-

bility. We are constantly re-imagining its reality" (*PS* 17). An instance of this re-imagining occurs near the end of *Let It Come
Down* as Nelson Dyar, the novel's central character, tries to enter
"a region of his memory" that will bring him momentary peace:

> He was covered by a patchwork quilt which was being tucked in
> securely on both sides—with his fingers he could feel the cross-
> stitching where the pieces were joined—and his head was lying on
> the eiderdown pillow his grandmother had made for him, the softest
> pillow he had ever felt. And like the sky, his mother was spread
> above him. . . . With his eyes closed there was nothing but his bed
> and her presence. Her voice was above, and she was all around; that
> way there was no possible danger in the world.[19]

His mind quickly snaps back to a rather less than peaceful present, but his need for a condition of security, perceived here as in
Bachelard as a primal human imperative, remains acute.

Dyar is in an extremely precarious position at this point in the
novel. He has stolen a large sum of money and is being taken in a
small boat to a hut in Spanish Morocco where he can hide from
the authorities. The house belongs to the family of his Moroccan
guide, Thami:

> It's a fort, thought Dyar, seeing the little structure crouching there
> atop its crazy pillar. Its thick earthen walls once had been partially
> whitewashed, and its steep roof, thatched in terraces, looked like a
> flounced petticoat of straw. The path led up, around, and out onto
> the promontory where the ground was bare save for a few over-
> grown bushes. There were no windows, but there was a patchwork
> door with a homemade lock, to fit which Thami now pulled from
> his pocket a heavy key as long as his hand. (*LD* 244)

This fortress-cottage in a desolate mountain area of a still primitive country resembles, especially in its protective function, the
"hermit's hut" to which Bachelard says we flee, in dreams, "in
search of real refuge" (*PS* 31). But Bowles' hut proves to be quite
the opposite of a refuge. Dyar, disturbed by the wind's banging
the loose front door, resolves to make it more secure because in
his mind the loose door is "equivalent to an open door. A little
piece of wood, a hammer and one nail could arrange everything:
the barrier between himself and the world outside would be
much more real" (*LD* 249). "Everything" proves difficult to ar-

range, however, and the world outside comes in with a vengeance. Before the novel concludes, Dyar, his mind clouded with
suspicion, fear, and hashish, uses the hammer to drive a nail
through Thami's ear while the Moroccan lies sleeping. For the
first time Dyar feels real and alive, no longer a passive victim, but
the crime he commits is horrible and the cloak of humanity he
casts aside, irretrievable.

Flimsy, ineffectual architectural structures can be found almost everywhere in Bowles' fiction. Sometimes buildings fail to
keep out danger (as in *Up Above the World*); sometimes they are
in a state of decay; sometimes they are torn down, plowed under,
or blown up. And sometimes they simply seem not to rest on secure foundations. In "A Distant Episode" the back room of a café
hangs "hazardously out above the river" (*CS* 40), while "The
Echo" takes place largely in a house perched precariously over a
ravine. One of Bowles' most recent stories, "In the Red Room,"
focuses on a house that, like the hut in *Let It Come Down*, has
been the setting for a murder. A young Sri Lankan takes three
Americans—a man who lives there and his visiting parents—to a
house he at first says is for sale. The place is in a state of dilapida-
tion. There is "no gate," the stables are "ruined," and the house
itself is "hidden by high bushes and flowering trees." They proceed "through a series of dark empty rooms" (*MM* 168) into one
that is painted entirely in crimson. After sitting there for a few
awkward minutes they leave, and the narrator later discovers that
on his wedding day the Sri Lankan had found his bride in that
room in bed with his best man. He shot them to death and
chopped up their bodies. Seldom in Bowles does an architectural
structure, in this case a home for newlyweds, so totally fail to
protect. "Here to Learn," another late story, takes Malika, a
naive Moroccan girl, from the security of her mother's house to a
Los Angeles mansion where she feels terribly out of place and
afraid. When she at last returns to Morocco, she finds that her
mother has died and the family house (which Malika never really
left imaginatively) has been demolished. More is signified at
the end of that story than the bulldozing of a house. Malika's
travels in Europe and America and her acquisition of great
wealth through marriage have been directed toward earning her
mother's approval. The parent/child axis is never very far from

the surface in Bowles. But her mother (as well as her husband) is dead, and Malika, though now a wealthy woman, is homeless.

Psychological, social, and religious shelters in Bowles impinge on one another and cannot be wholly separated. They are all part of what Peter Berger calls the *nomos,* or order, established by human beings as "a shield against terror." Berger argues that man, because he is "biologically denied the ordering mechanisms with which the other animals are endowed, is compelled to impose his own order upon experience." We do this in a ceaseless attempt to make a stubbornly nonhuman world appear sufficiently human for us to live in it. The *nomos* we construct is "an area of meaning carved out of a vast mass of meaninglessness, a small clearing of lucidity in a formless, dark, always ominous jungle." Like Bowles, Berger recognizes that "every socially constructed *nomos* must face the constant possibility of its collapse into anomy." The result can be submersion of the individual "in a world of disorder, senselessness, and madness."[20] Since human identity, as Berger sees it, is socially shaped, the ultimate danger to the individual in such a collapse is the loss of a sense of selfhood. Social structures in Bowles are wide-ranging and various. Their common denominator is that they do tend to collapse, leaving people who need their protection on the outside.

The failure of shelter plays itself out on different levels in Bowles' fiction. There is the level of broad cultural conflict, when one *nomos* meets another—a subject I address in Chapter 3. There are also more intimate social collapses, and these are no less catastrophic for involving only one, two, or three people. We have already taken note of several of them. Malika's sense of place and personal identity are destroyed at the end of "Here to Learn." Driss' uncles, far from providing adequate protection, are the first to perish in "The Delicate Prey." The young Sri Lankan of "In the Red Room" keeps the murder chamber as "a sort of shrine" (*MM* 174) to remind him of what he has lost. And the woman who waits for her fiancé in "How Many Midnights" finally has only the cold winter wind for a companion. The difficulty of knowing another person, the difficulty of feeling safe within the structure of any human relationship, and the intuition of an intractable foreignness everywhere one turns must be seen in personal terms before they can be seen in cultural or political terms.

Many of Bowles' plots move toward epiphanies in which characters recognize their outsidedness. In the most effective stories their sense of alienation is rendered with quiet yet intense dramatic skill. "The Echo" is one of these tales of agonizing personal estrangement. Familial interiors, as the derivation of the word *familial* suggests, should be the most familiar of all. But, as in "The Frozen Fields," the real threat, the most resolutely *un*familiar, is already within the house. The story opens with Aileen, an American college student, flying down to Colombia to visit her mother during spring break. Several unusual and discordant aspects of the situation quickly become evident. Although Aileen thinks she is "going to a new home" (*CS* 51), a letter from her mother indicates that the home will not be very secure for her. Before returning to an old family house in Colombia, the mother has apparently taken up with a younger woman, a sculptress named Prue, and Aileen clearly does not approve of the relationship. The pattern is similar to that in "Reminders of Bouselham" except that here the denouement is more violent and the victory of the usurper, more final.

Even before arriving at the house, Aileen has uneasy feelings about the gorge near which it stands: "She had no memory of the gorge. . . . However, she had a clear memory of its presence, of the sensation of enormous void beyond and below the side of the house" (*CS* 53). Already the house takes shape as a sign of safety, and the void as emblematic of all that lies just beyond the realm of safety. It is therefore significant that Aileen falls into a small ditch shortly before her mother and Prue meet her to take her home. The fall prefigures Aileen's entry into a greater void at the end of the story.

When she takes up residence with her mother and Prue, Aileen asks "to be put into the old part of the house, rather than into a more comfortable room in the new wing" (*CS* 56). The new wing, "built right out over the gorge" (*CS* 52), seems insubstantial to Aileen, but it is the area of the compound that is most intimately a part of her mother's new (and to Aileen, unpleasant) domestic arrangement. During one of several confrontations with

Prue, Aileen asks, "Are you planning on staying long?" and Prue
replies, "What the hell do you mean? . . . I live here" (*CS* 57).
Shortly afterward Aileen's mother pleads with her to be more polite to Prue, and she refers to them both as her "guests." This
conversation marks an important stage in Aileen's decline; the
more she feels "outside," the more unstable her personality
becomes.

A few days later, while on a long walk, Aileen comes upon a
young Colombian standing on the other side of a barbed wire
fence, the starkest twentieth-century emblem for the division between outside and inside. He spits in her face and she responds,
after he retreats into a hut, by flinging a stone at him and apparently hitting her target. His cry, significant, has "the indignation
and outraged innocence of a small baby," although it is also "a
grown man's cry" (*CS* 59). Returning to her mother's house, she
becomes increasingly disoriented: "She was horrified to see how
near she stood to the ugly black edge of the gorge. And the house
looked insane down there, leaning out over as if it were trying to
see the bottom" (*CS* 59). These images build and reflect on one
another as the story approaches its climax: the hut that fails
to protect the youth from Aileen's stone, the deterioration of
Aileen's structure of self, the house that is not a home reaching
out futilely over the void. Aileen does not enter that void until
after her mother orders her to leave. On the day of her departure
the tension between her and Prue breaks into a furious physical
brawl, with Aileen beating and kicking the other woman. Aileen
then utters "the greatest scream of her life" (*CS* 63), and the
scream, which replays the earlier cry of the young man, echoes
hollowly back from across the gorge. The scream originates in
her momentary understanding of the awesome dimensions of
solitude. As she descends the trail and looks back to see her
mother and Prue standing together on the terrace of the house,
the only shelter she can find is that of a "deep dream" (*CS* 63).
The anguish of rejection is an emotion that Bowles always con-
veys with haunting clarity. Aileen is truly an outsider wishing she
could be in.

A closer look at "How Many Midnights" reveals similar patterns of imagery and meaning. Here, too, the architecture of human relationships is precarious, and here, too, a young woman

finds herself shut out. The woman, June, lives with her parents but for two years has been dating a man named Van, whom she plans to marry in ten days. During those two years nothing has "occurred between them which was not what her parents would call 'honorable'" (*CS* 103). The story takes place on the first night she intends to spend with Van. He has given her the keys to his apartment for the first time, and she waits for him there. Her sense of her relationship with Van as a kind of construct is quickly established and linked to the cozy interior of the apartment, which she has redecorated to make it more familiar to her—to make it "her space," in today's vernacular.

June's knowledge of the apartment is emphasized with quiet insistence—she even knows how many steps are in each flight of stairs leading up to it—but her knowledge of Van himself is called into question at every turn. This is important because although June succeeds in making Van's "place" hers, she does so ultimately at the price of making it no longer his. One of the earliest indications of June's failure to know Van is her reflection on an incident that took place the night before at the bookshop where Van works. Van was outside the shop inspecting a window display he had just completed, when he saw a man inside secreting a book in his overcoat. Van quickly found a policeman, and the shoplifter was arrested. The incident strikes June as "sinister." She thinks Van was "unfair," at least partly owing to her involuntary identification with the thief. June's reaction is instructive. She does not consciously understand that in redoing Van's apartment and rearranging his life in countless other ways, she is indeed a kind of thief, robbing him of the interior that *he* has constructed to make *himself* feel comfortable. But she does grasp that Van's response to a situation might not always be the same as hers, and she is bothered by that element of surprise in his behavior. Surprise is inimical to domestication, whose aim is to make the strange seem familiar and predictable.

As the hour grows later and Van does not arrive at the apartment, June decides to rearrange the furniture in the living room. The project is partly a desperate attempt to stave off panic and partly an effort to complete the transformation of Van's place into her own. During the move a drawer drops out of a small chest, spilling a number of letters. She frantically tries to get the letters back into the drawer in their original configuration; she fears that "Van might think she had been reading his correspondence" (*CS* 106). She is afraid because closed drawers constitute, as Bachelard says, "a model of intimacy." A wardrobe's inner space, he continues, speaking of all such structures, is "*intimate space, space that is not open to just anybody*" (*PS* 78). In that enclosed structure "there exists a center of order that protects the entire house against uncurbed disorder" (*PS* 79). But the intimacy and the order here are Van's, and June senses that she has violated them. This is the point at which she begins to feel *herself* a violation, an intruder. But still she clings to the interior she has fashioned: "The candles had burned down half way; she looked at them, at the ivy trailing down from the little pots on the wall, at the white goatskin by her feet, at the striped curtains. They were all hers. 'Van, Van,' she said under her breath" (*CS* 109). Shortly afterward she falls asleep. When she awakens, she thinks she sees Van "moving slowly across the floor toward the window," then reaching up to "swing himself through the window" (*CS* 110). Her discovery that his overnight valise is missing confirms that Van has resisted domestication, has become part of her outside. While there may not be, as Johannes Bertens complains, an overt explanation for Van's behavior, the reasons for it are implicit on every page and are, in fact, rather obvious. The foreignness of that which should be most familiar is a major strain in Bowles' work. In this story it plays itself out with inexorable intensity, as June goes in a cab first to the river's edge, "her whole life falling to pieces before her" (*CS* 111), then back to her parents' apartment: "When she had undressed she opened the big window without looking out, and got into bed. The cold wind blew through the room" (*CS* 111). There seems little difference now between inside and out.

A recently published fragment by Bowles—the initial section of a novel he never completed—also focuses on sexual foreignness as a basic problem in human experience. This piece is shaped by two of Bowles' favorite plot elements: a voyage to a place that, whatever else it is, must be defined as not-home; and a widening circle of estrangement that can be defined as a failure to reach out and bring the other into one's domain. The entire fragment takes place on board a ship bound for the orient. The main

characters, Thorny (a name that intrigued Bowles) and Anne
Sims, are on their way to occupy a house that Thorny has rented
in Ceylon. The energy of the story derives from two distinct but
closely related motifs that alternate with each other throughout.
One has to do with Anne's gathering feeling of discomfort as
home is left farther and farther behind. The other, more dramatically insistent, concerns her alienation from Thorny. The voyage
to Ceylon is not Anne's idea of a good time. The weather is sultry,
the sea is too rough, the food is terrible, and the other people on
board the ship are boorish. She is unimpressed by the tropics,
"unbearably hot and exhausting, without a shred of beauty or
subtlety." [21] She wants "to slide through the whole experience of
the trip without having to consider it objectively" (*LC* 67).

To this end she takes Dramamine, but the stupor that the drug
induces is also meant to help her avoid facing her husband, who,
after ten years, is more of a stranger to her than ever. The Dramamine places her in a "protective fog" that makes "discussions
less possible" (*LC* 67). She adds to that protection by keeping to
herself whenever she can. She hopes that Thorny will stay in their
cabin a little longer so that she may sit alone in the bar, un-
disturbed by his presence. Having all but given up any attempt to
bring Thorny into her sphere of familiarity, she settles for shutting him out. If the alien cannot be domesticated, it must be
blocked off, banished. What is so subversive about Bowles is that
the alien is frequently this close to home. Anne reflects that she is
"less sure" (*LC* 68) about her husband than when they first met;
and she recalls that he never can understand when she is angered
and disappointed by his behavior. As soon as he does arrive in
the bar, their strained relations become evident, even to a somewhat obtuse English couple with whom they are sitting. They argue about what she will wear to dinner, but this is obviously not
the underlying cause of the conflict. When she finally agrees
to return to the cabin to change clothes, she does so "with unexpected vehemence" (*LC* 70)—unexpected because the ultimate implications of their unfamiliarity with one another remain
partly, and deliberately, hidden. She admits that she stays with
Thorny out of "habit" (*LC* 70); what she fails to admit is that the
habit originates in a fear of being even more alone than she feels
with him.

A passage near the end of the story further elucidates Anne's problem. Reading the works of Simone Weil provides her "with the kind of reassurance and comfort that ordinarily is forthcoming only from contact with the living person rather than the printed page" (*LC* 70). This is clearly a substitute for the shelter of a human relationship, which is failing her. But even reading is narcotic, a "protective fog." When she reads she does not progressively project her imagination over new territories of text; instead, she circles the same safe areas repeatedly, as if to reassert her control over this one small, inviolable domain. When Thorny enters the cabin, he comes as the outsider he is, disturbing her tranquility. The story ends with the situation in a state of delicate equilibrium, with conflicting signals from Anne: "Oh shut up" and the more conciliatory "Are you coming to dinner?" (*LC* 71). Bowles' manuscript notes make it clear that the conflict between Anne and Thorny will worsen after they reach Ceylon until a complete rupture occurs. One line in particular reveals the extent of Anne's alienation: "She admits that she equates being with him and being alone, and solitude in a strange place is her idea of hell." [22]

"Call at Corazón," written earlier than the fragment, addresses the same questions with an economy that is almost brutal. This story, too, moves along a path of expanding awareness of estrangement between a husband and a wife. The couple are on a honeymoon trip, largely a river voyage, in a backwater region of Latin America. The first source of discord is a monkey the husband wants to buy and install in their cabin. The beast is a fitting representative of the outside world that resists domestication, and the argument it causes is the occasion for the couple's mutual recognition that they are not familiar with each other. The ensuing exchange forcefully dramatizes the degree of their estrangement. The woman tries to enclose: "I'm still talking to you. I expect you to be crazy, and I expect to give in to you all along. I'm crazy too, I know. But I wish there were some way I could just once feel that my giving in meant anything to you. I wish you knew how to be gracious about it" (*CS* 65). But the effort fails; her husband declines to be drawn in. No real communication occurs, and no social enclosure is erected. A few lines later the woman gives up, saying, "Don't talk to me. . . . Go and

buy your monkey" (*CS* 66). Her sudden acquiescence is a sign of
defeat. She wants only to shut off conversation, and to ensure
that result she insists, "I'd love to have it. I really would. I think
it's sweet" (*CS* 66). He buys the monkey immediately, although
he knows it is really against her wishes. Not long afterward he
finds the monkey "on his bunk, slowly tearing the pages from the
book he had been reading" (*CS* 67)—another sign of the collapse of the structures that comprise the human sense of an interior. "The storm in the sky," "the falling rain" (*CS* 67), an open
porthole, and a boat described as an "old tub" (*CS* 69) further
suggest a potentially dangerous outside and a precarious
enclosure.

After changing to a second boat (the "old tub") to continue
the journey, the couple resume their quarreling. Their repeated
failure to connect conversationally with each other is reminiscent
of similar situations in Hemingway, particularly in "Hills like
White Elephants," a favorite of Bowles and the first Hemingway
he ever read.[23] But as Millicent Dillon has observed, "Call at Corazón" and other stories of tension between men and women
probably have a more direct source in Bowles' own life.[24] Paul
and Jane Bowles spent their honeymoon in Central America and,
like the couple in "Call at Corazón," they acquired a pet along
the way:

> We bought a parrot on the way back to Puntarenas, ingenuously
> imagining that since it had a chain attached to its leg, it could be left
> more or less anywhere. It proved us wrong while we were still on
> the ferry and continued to wreak havoc even after it had destroyed
> and escaped from its third cage. (*WS* 209)

But Bowles goes on to say that "life had gone smoothly" in Central America. "Jane and I never argued, never grew tired of being
together" (*WS* 210). It was only later, in Paris, where Jane had
other friends, that problems began to develop. The independent
life that Jane led there increasingly troubled Paul. "Call at Corazón" weaves these disparate elements together into a fictional
web that stands apart from but is clearly related to the author's
own experience. In the story a complete rupture takes place. The
husband, having awakened from a long nap, finds his wife on
deck, in a drunken stupor, lying only half-dressed beside a native

man. As in "How Many Midnights," the obstinate refusal of the other to be familiar brings about a denouement. The husband leaves the boat, goes into the port of call, and boards a train, leaving his bride behind. As the train pulls away he thinks he sees her running toward the station. Unperturbed, he places his notebook on his lap and watches the landscape move "with increasing speed past the window" (*CS* 75). He has made her a part of his outside as completely as Van does June in "How Many Midnights." For the time being, the new interior he has constructed is under his control, safe. An entry in his notebook could be the epigraph for all of Bowles' fiction: "Frightfulness is never more than an unfamiliar pattern" (*CS* 66).

"The Hours after Noon," one of Bowles' longer stories, is also one of his most effective dramatizations of the frightfulness inherent in unfamiliar patterns. The mind's efforts to impose familiar patterns on reality generate much of the story's action. The theme is first struck in an epigraph from Baudelaire: "If one could awaken all the echoes of one's memory simultaneously, they would make a music, delightful or sad as the case might be, but logical and without dissonances. No matter how incoherent the existence, the human unity is not affected" (*CS* 217). This passage, as it applies to "The Hours after Noon," strongly suggests that the human construction of reality is indeed possible— that a human unity can be fashioned out of existential chaos. Bowles himself, in a conversation with Lawrence Stewart, seems to endorse that positive reading, explaining Baudelaire's words as "an affirmation of . . . the power of the subjective side of the personality. Because it's the same consciousness taking all these things in, no matter how disparate they all are, the memory will be harmonious because they all happened to you and you saw them all" (*PB* 81–82). This pattern-making power, as I shall discuss in a later chapter, is essential both to survival in the world and to defining our humanity, but it has its limits. The epigraph begins, after all, with the word "if," and the narrative that follows is largely a commentary on the cautious subjunctivity of the "affirmation."

The story opens with a very human, very familiar ceremony— mealtime at Pension Callender, a small Tangier establishment run by an American and his wife. Even within this civilized structure, however, fear of the outside, the unfamiliar, intrudes. The Callenders are momentarily expecting the arrival of a new guest, Monsieur Royer, who has an unsavory reputation. They are also expecting the arrival of their daughter, Charlotte, who is coming for a visit during her school's holidays. Monsieur Royer is the primary source of danger, in Mrs. Callender's eyes. He is the ambassador extraordinary of the world outside who will burst in upon the pension and cause unimaginable harm. That the harm is unimaginable, or at least unutterable, makes it seem all the more frightful. The reader later learns that Royer is dangerous, but not to Charlotte Callender. Royer explains to her, quite casually, that "there are a great many girls who have no will, like the natives here, or even the Spanish girls of the lower class." There is no question of "ruining" such girls: "It is all the same to them, as long as they receive a gift" (*CS* 233). Royer makes it plain that Charlotte is in a different category entirely. She is safe. For her, the sexual danger comes from another of the pension's guests, the archeologist Mr. Van Siclen, whom Mrs. Callender foolishly trusts and even admires.

Mrs. Callender's growing feeling of discomfort and her consequent attempt to keep Charlotte and Royer apart lead to the story's grisly climax. She induces Van Siclen to invite Royer to accompany him on a dig for a few days. Meanwhile, Charlotte visits an old lycée friend who lives nearby and is unable to reach her parents on the telephone to tell them she will be late. Mrs. Callender, learning that her daughter has been seen in Van Siclen's car, goes out to look for her. At the dig Van Siclen tells her that he has not seen Charlotte since morning and that Royer is also missing. Mrs. Callender and Van Siclen discover nothing when they search for the absent couple (who are not together at all), but in a final vignette the narrator discloses that Royer has been murdered while on the verge of molesting a young Moroccan girl. Since arriving in Tangier Royer has tried unsuccessfully to remember a favorite line from Gide, "*Le temps qui coule ici n'a plus d'heures, mais, tant l'inoccupation de chacun est parfaite, ici devient impossible l'ennui.*" [25] As he holds the girl on his lap in the moonlight, he is finally about to recall the whole sentence. That the recollection is interrupted by sudden, unexpected death is perhaps more significant than the languor and emptiness the passage evokes. Like that of the Moungari in "The Delicate Prey," Royer's attempt at articulation is cut off. The story's last line, "This time he might have completed it" (*CS* 242), echoes the conditional sense of the Baudelaire epigraph and reasserts the contingency of human constructs, including conceptual ones. What happens to Royer is typical of the disasters that befall many Bowles characters who find themselves without the shelter of familiar patterns. "The Hours after Noon" begins amid the cozy yet precarious familiarity of a luncheon and ends with a brutal killing "in the empty countryside" (*CS* 242). Royer's fate, utter annihilation, reveals the existence of an awful, comprehensive danger of which sexual assault is only one manifestation.

The entire story is pervaded by that sense of general menace, even while seeming to focus on Mrs. Callender's specific fear of Royer and Charlotte's specific fear of Van Siclen. The greater threat is from the world outside, which can at any moment eradicate all vestiges of human unity. Mrs. Callender, looking at that terrifying structureless world out a Bowlesian window, almost grasps the truth:

> As a rule the mornings took care of themselves; it was the hours after noon that she had to beware of, when the day had begun to go toward the night, and she no longer trusted herself to be absolutely certain of what she would do next, or of what unlikely idea would come into her head. Once again she peered between the curtains up the sunlit path, but there was nobody. (*CS* 222)

What Mrs. Callender dimly fears is the absence of certainty and control implicit in a familiar pattern. (One of the unlikely, and quite unacceptable, ideas that come into her head is the notion of her own sexual attraction to Van Siclen, a feeling which she cannot control and therefore fears.) Her gazing through a window is important, because what terrifies her lies outside the rational, conscious self, outside "the power of the subjective side of the personality" that can construct and defend such a self.

The pension is the visible sign of Mrs. Callender's construction of that human unity which constitutes home, in the profoundest sense. The pension is a fortress to her; it is her casbah. Of the Moroccans she says, "One never knows what any of them will take it into his head to do next" (*CS* 220). This is, of course, precisely what she fears in herself, but she manages most of the time to couch it in social or cultural terms. Moroccans are unpredictable, strange; Royer is "a confirmed roué and a scoundrel" (*CS* 234). In each case the danger is placed safely outside. She spares no pains to strengthen her enclosures against that outside. Though she was born in Gibraltar of "an English father and a Spanish mother," she considers herself "English through and through," and she determines to make her daughter "a typical English girl" (*CS* 219). Much of her sexual anxiety, both for herself and for Charlotte, derives from a dread of the moral laxness that she considers foreign rather than English. But her carefully wrought conception of home (and of her own safe, predictable English identity) is ineluctably undermined by the fact that she is an exile making an artificial home in a foreign place.

Mrs. Callender's fear of the outside is nowhere more forcefully rendered than in a scene in which she hears a distant Moroccan melody:

> A *rhaïta* was being played fairly far away on the mountain, announcing a wedding. It would probably go on for several days and nights. She put her hands over her ears. As if that could help! Whenever she took them away, the slippery little sound would be there, twisting thinly around itself like a tree-snake. She pressed her palms more tightly against her head, until the vacuum hurt her eardrums. But the images had been awakened: the donkeys laden with blankets and painted wooden chests, the procession of lanterns, the native women in white with their drums. . . . (*CS* 236)

Putting her hands over her ears is Mrs. Callender's way of shutting the window, but the world outside will not be so easily closed off. The larger dimension of danger is evident in the occasional blending of the song with an even more alien noise: "The wind still blew, the trees still swayed and roared, and through their sound from time to time crept the shrill, tiny notes of the distant *rhaïta*" (*CS* 239). Although what she hears is a humanly built interior (a wedding song, after all), it is one that Mrs. Callender cannot enter, so for her it represents the frightful external. But unfamiliarity, like danger, is a relative thing in Bowles' fiction. The threat of either Royer's or Van Siclen's sexual advances seems minor in comparison to Royer's total destruction at the end of the story; and the unintelligibility of the *rhaïta* seems almost a familiar pattern next to the inarticulate and indifferent howling of the wind.

2. Interiors and Exteriors (II)

BOWLES' NOVELS make extensive and various use of architectural metaphor. *The Spider's House* is an appropriate place to begin a closer examination of those longer narratives since, as its title indicates, the idea of architectural form is its focal point. The novel is a meticulously detailed portrait of a rapidly disintegrating traditional society—a society that has functioned as a "house" for its inhabitants for centuries. The disintegration is seen through the eyes of Amar, an unschooled Moroccan boy living in Fez, and John Stenham, an American expatriate novelist (and sometime author-surrogate) who briefly befriends him. The action occurs in the spring and summer of 1954, during the period just before independence, when the French, in a desperate attempt to hold onto the Protectorate, kidnapped and exiled the popular nationalistic sultan, Sidi Mohammed. Amar and Stenham do not meet until near the novel's chronological end (August 1954), when the French responded to riots and terrorism by closing the walled medina, imprisoning those inside and locking out everyone else, including Amar, who is unable to get back to his father's house and must depend on Stenham, a "Nazarene," for protection. That protection is undependable, however. At the end of the book both Stenham and his lady friend Lee Burroughs are off to the safer city of Casablanca ("white house"), leaving Amar standing alone in an empty road.

The idea of architectural form first suggests protection in a purely literal sense. The medina, or old city, of Fez is described as a vast interior with many chambers and many wrong turns surrounded by a wall. But even this interiority is illusory, since the vacant sky can be seen above the city's narrow streets. And the idea of protection quickly assumes broader significance. Stenham, speaking of the Moroccans, says, "Any building's a refuge,

something to get inside of and really *feel* inside, and that means it
has to be dark. They hate windows. It's only when they've shut
themselves in that they can relax. The whole world outside is
hostile and dangerous."[1] That protective purpose is presented
here as primarily an exclusionary effort; the dangerous exterior
is kept out. Again and again in the novel the outside is hazardous, irrational, chaotic, as when Amar, Stenham, and Lee take
cover in a café during a riot: "Two waiters were sliding enormous
bolts across the closed entrance door" (*SH* 255). A few minutes
later, after a general slaughter begins, everyone who can reaches
"some sort of shelter" until there is "no one . . . left outside but
the soldiers" (*SH* 257). But the effort to enclose is even more important than the effort to exclude, for the space that is inside was
once out; it is exterior space domesticated, brought into the
house. This profounder function of architectural form (profounder because it implies transformation, not just exclusion) can
be readily seen in the typical Arabic enclosed courtyard, with its
greenery (cultivated, not wild) and its carefully contained running
water or fountain: the outdoors brought in, the wild made tame.

If domestication is the goal, it is seldom fully achieved in
Bowles. In *The Spider's House,* as in the other novels and the
stories, neither house nor family seems to be secure enough. At
the beginning of the book Stenham emerges from the home of a
Moroccan family after a long, traditional dinner. At that time the
house and the family within it seem models of safety, but later, as
partisan violence escalates throughout the Protectorate, the
house falls apart: "Several tons of rubble lay piled up at one end:
stones, earth, and plaster. The wall of the house across the street
was visible through the gaping hole" (*SH* 219). Si Jaffar, the head
of the household and Stenham's friend, insists that rain caused
the wall to collapse. But more likely, the house was bombed by
the pro-independence Istiqlal. If so, the family within, who are
suspected of collaborating with the French, are no safer than the
building that inadequately protects them.

Amar seeks shelter a number of times; in fact, he almost continuously moves from one insufficient shelter to another. Early in
the novel he encounters Moulay Ali, a member of the Istiqlal,
who takes him to his house and keeps him there several hours.

Because he is held prisoner until Moulay Ali and his associates can determine that he is not working for the other side, Amar is impressed by the house's security, although he does not want his life linked with Moulay Ali's. Much later, however, when he is locked out of the medina, cannot contact his family, and has been separated from Stenham, he is forced to seek Moulay Ali's assistance. Moulay Ali promises to send for word of Amar's relatives, and does so. Amar's mother and sister have fled to the home of an older sister in Meknès, a nearby city. Amar stays at Moulay Ali's house into the night, playing the *lirah*, a kind of flute, for Moulay Ali and his guests. But during this period of relative comfort and serenity, Moulay Ali and his people, having heard the house is about to be raided, slip away, leaving Amar behind to face the alien French alone. The crickets "singing outside the window" (*SH* 372) bespeak a calm that does not last. The French burst in, "breaking the windows," and the crickets' singing gives way to the "brittle music" (*SH* 398) of glass shattering on the ground. Amar escapes, but he knows that the house belongs "completely to what had been and never would be again" (*SH* 400). And he understands, too, that from this time on "nothing would have meaning, because the knowing was itself the meaning; beyond that there was nothing to know" (*SH* 399).

Social structures are linked to physical ones in *The Spider's House* through the medium of Fez itself. The city, like the individual house, is an architectural form. There is frequent talk in the novel of the importance of being inside or outside the walls, of the medina's being open or closed, of being either trapped inside or shut out. What emerges from all this talk is a growing sense of the vulnerability both of the old city and of the traditional society it embodies: "Slowly he walked up to the big gate and passed under its main arch, out into the world of motors and exhaust fumes" (*SH* 133). Modernization is a grave danger not only to the physical Fez but to the idea that gives it meaning— "the Moslem code of justice" and Islamic tradition in general: "Beyond the gates of justice lay the world of savages, *kaffirine*, wild beasts" (*SH* 116). Bowles suggests other types of social structures but dismisses their effectiveness rather abruptly. Speaking of a friend of hers, Lee tells Stenham that he first joined the

Communist Party, later "went in for Yoga," and finally became a Roman Catholic. "That didn't stop him," she concludes, "from getting to be an alcoholic" (*SH* 239).

Bowles is not simply an apologist (as his character Stenham tries to be) for the old Moroccan way of life, however, and *The Spider's House* is more than an indictment of western civilization. The point is that *all* human shelters are flimsy. This subject can best be approached by looking at Amar, who is, apart from his own father, the novel's most loyal Moslem. Amar is genuinely shocked by his encounters with Moslems who drink alcohol or in some other way step "beyond the gates," yet he himself, without fully realizing it, is moving in that direction. He desperately wants, for instance, a pair of European shoes. He feels protected by his knowledge that his world is no longer "the immutable world of law, the written word" (*SH* 29) in which his father believes, but in fact his own sense of assurance, that feeling of protection, is derived from the security of tradition (his father's house, essentially), and as that structure gradually deteriorates, he finds "the whole vast . . . live, mysterious earth" (*SH* 29) increasingly more terrifying than romantic. Most significantly, the event on which the novel's entire plot hinges, the meeting of Amar and Stenham, occurs in a café *outside* the walls of the city. Amar's attaching himself to Stenham, an outsider in every sense of the word, is a momentous choice for him—a conscious step, rather than a subconscious drift, outward. He really has no alternative, of course. By this time, during the revolutionary turmoil of August 1954, the old, safe, walled-in way of life is so rapidly collapsing that even for people like Amar, there soon will be no inside left.

Social ties between individuals are no more dependable in *The Spider's House* than in Bowles' other work. Stenham and Lee, for example, do leave Fez together at the end of the novel and appear to be in love, but in most respects the trajectory of their relationship is similar to those of the couples in "Call at Corazón" and "How Many Midnights." Nothing in their getting together suggests very strongly that they will be able to stay together. Each character, like those in the stories, inhabits a self-created "inside," and each tries to draw the other in. Stenham, with his atheist upbringing and his disenchantment with the Communist

Party (to which he, like Bowles, belonged briefly), has none of the more common conceptual materials with which to fashion his personal interior. After leaving the Party he withdrew "into a subjectivity which refused existence to any reality or law but its own. . . . Nothing had importance save the exquisitely isolated cosmos of his own consciousness" (*SH* 195). Gradually he became aware that even this construct had no meaning and so fell back "upon the mere reflex action of living, the automatic getting through the day that had to be done if one were to retain any semblance of sanity" (*SH* 196).

This is the condition in which Stenham finds himself when he meets Lee Burroughs. But Stenham's strong suit is self-deception, and he has in fact a more complicated system of shelters than merely "getting through the day." Part of that system involves an urge to go *beyond* the conventional forms of protection (which are correctly perceived to be unstable) and construct a new, wholly self-created shelter, on the "outside." Consider this passage, the conclusion of a long rumination on the city of Fez:

> It was all these strange and lonely spots outside the walls, where the city-dwellers unanimously advised him not to walk, that he loved. Yet their beauty existed for him only to the degree that he was conscious of their outsidedness. . . . It was the knowledge that the swarming city lay below, shut in by its high ramparts, which made wandering over the hills and along the edges of the cliffs so delectable. They are there, of it, he would think, and I am here, of nothing, free. (*SH* 166)

Stenham's predilection for these external places springs from the same impulse that motivates him and many other Bowles characters to sojourn in distant lands. One defense against the open window is to pass through it, survive, and create a new, familiar space outside. But Stenham's need for detachment has another source, too. He fears change and therefore believes

> that a man must at all costs keep some part of himself outside and beyond life. If he should ever for an instant cease doubting, accept wholly the truth of what his senses conveyed to him, he would be dislodged from the solid ground to which he clung and swept along with the current, having lost all objective sense, totally involved in existence. (*SH* 203)

Stenham is "plagued by the suspicion that someday he would discover he had always been wrong" (*SH* 203–204) about this belief; and indeed, that outside ground on which he stands does prove to be less than solid, as he drifts into gradually increasing involvement with Lee, with Amar, and, much against his will, with the quickly changing political events of that summer.

Stenham's fear of change is evident in his romanticizing of Morocco and his opposition to modernization, and this is the point at which his self-created interior, his sense of his world, most dramatically conflicts with Lee's. Stenham's vision of Fez's future is grim:

> A few bombs would transform its delicate hand-molded walls into piles of white dust; it would no longer be the enchanted labyrinth sheltered from time, where as he wandered mindlessly, what his eyes saw told him that he had at last found the way back. When this city fell, the past would be finished. The thousand-year gap would be bridged in a split second, as the first bomb thundered. (*SH* 167)

The whole country would become, Stenham tells Lee, "just a huge European slum, full of poverty and hatred" (*SH* 188). This fear makes comprehensible both Stenham's temporary "adoption" of Amar and his subsequent abandonment of the boy. His enthusiasm for Amar is occasioned by his mistaken notion that Amar is a pure representative of an unspoiled Morocco—a Morocco that has already ceased to exist except in Stenham's imagination.

Lee's conception of Morocco is quite the opposite of Stenham's, but it is no less an idealization, since she envisions the evolution of a sort of Maghrebi Scandinavia. She calls Stenham's point of view not only that of "an outsider" but, more damningly, of "a tourist who puts picturesqueness above everything else" (*SH* 188). She insists that the Moroccans must welcome "the hospitals and electric lights and buses the French have brought" (*SH* 188). Stenham reflects that *this* is surely the remark of a tourist, and his esteem for Lee lessens. Later Stenham wonders why such a young and attractive woman should take an interest in Morocco or even be in that country at a time of such tension. His conclusion, that she is a Communist agent, proves false, but it demonstrates the extent to which his imagination will go to make an unfamiliar pattern seem familiar. For her part, Lee has read Stenham's novels and romanticized (familiarized) *him*. In a letter to a friend she writes, "I had imagined someone so utterly different, someone more decided and less neurotic, more understanding and less petulant. I feel terribly let down. You could say he means well, I suppose, but he's so clumsy and moody and calculating, all at the same time, that a little of him goes a long way" (*SH* 298). In another letter she calls him "ineffectual . . . soft. . . . reactionary and opinionated" (*SH* 299). Their mutual antagonism continues almost until the end of the novel. When a reconciliation does take place, it is not particularly convincing. They become lovers, but nothing in the novel suggests that they have really ceased being strangers to one another. Stenham and Lee are last seen (by Amar and by the reader) in an automobile bound for Casablanca. Their abrupt rejection of Amar, who does not fit into their newly slapped-together arrangement, bodes ill for their capacity to venture emotionally into truly alien territory.

The title of *The Spider's House*, with its obvious architectural reference, is important because its sources expand the metaphor further, from the personal, social, and political to the metaphysical. According to Bowles' epigraph from the Koran, "The likeness of those who choose other patrons than Allah is as the likeness of the spider when she taketh unto herself a house, and lo! the frailest of all houses is the spider's house, if they but knew." But Bowles implies that all houses are spider's houses. All humanly made structures, whether built of stone or of ideas, are transitory. None is safe. Stenham thinks to himself that mankind's most commendable accomplishment may well be "the inventing of gods in whom its members could wholly believe, and believing, thereby find life more bearable" (*SH* 198). Stenham himself, of course, does not believe. Amar does, yet he finds his own religious shelter in jeopardy when he hears that the French have beaten and imprisoned the *ulema* of the Karouine mosque, even though the holy men had taken sanctuary in the shrine of Moulay Idris. This news only confirms what Amar's employer has told him earlier in the novel: "It doesn't matter what anyone does now. Sins are finished!" (*SH* 44). And his father, not long afterward, said, "This is the end of Islam. . . . There is sin everywhere now" (*SH* 121). The two statements, Amar realizes, coin-

cide. Even Dar el-Islam, the House of the Islam, as Moslems call
their faith,[2] is not invulnerable.

Religion, as Peter Berger points out, is the ultimate stage of domestication. It is man's most comprehensive attempt to feel safe
by enclosing the entire world outside: "Religion implies the far-
thest reach of man's self-externalization, of his infusion of reality
with his own meanings. Religion implies that human order is
projected into the totality of being" (*SC* 27–28). Through religion, meaning is extended from the integrated self to an inte-
grated cosmos. The trend toward secularization casts doubt on
the very existence of that order. The growth of secular thinking,
and the danger it presents to traditional Islamic ways, is one of
the major themes of *The Spider's House*. Amar is scandalized
to see members of the Istiqlal drink alcohol and neglect their
prayers before meals, yet even he regards many of his father's
ideas as outmoded. Throughout most of the novel, however,
Amar remains convinced that the house of Islam will stand. Explaining his conception of the afterlife to Stenham, he uses words
like "place" and "inside" (*SH* 277) to indicate his belief that religion is a protective structure (despite clear signs of its crumbling)
and that the absolute shelter, the eternal interior, is paradise.
Bowles' own view of the matter more closely approximates the
pessimism and relativism of a passage he quotes from *The Thousand and One Nights*: "I have understood that the world is a vast
emptiness built upon emptiness. . . . And so they call me the
master of wisdom. Alas! Does anyone know what wisdom is?"
(*SH* 13).

The Sheltering Sky focuses even more sharply on human exteriority. Almost every detail in the book subverts the ostensible
meaning of its title, as shelter after shelter turns to emptiness
built upon emptiness. A folk story told early in the novel epitomizes this movement from interior to exterior and in doing so
reflects in small the novel's overall plot. In the parable three girls
from the mountains want more than anything to have tea in the
Sahara. After many months they amass enough money for a
journey into the Algerian desert. Walking from dune to dune
they at last find a suitable spot to impose their little ceremony
upon the wilderness. Days later a caravan passes. The three girls

are dead, and their glasses (like the Moungari's mouth in "The Delicate Prey") are filled with sand. The novel's main characters, who are traveling in the desert in an effort to spark some life into their increasingly strained marriage, have their tea in the Sahara in much the same way. Port Moresby,[3] struck down by typhoid in an isolated town, wanders first out of reason, then out of life. His wife Kit's mind disintegrates more gradually. At several stages of their journey she gazes at her "things" to remind herself that she is still a civilized, rational creature—that she is still "inside" a world whose furnishings and symbols are familiar and intelligible to her. When she spreads out her dresses, shoes, and toiletries, the significant contents of the enclosed domain of her luggage, it amuses the cynical Port "to watch her building her pathetic little fortress of Western culture in the middle of the wilderness."[4] Somewhat later, clutching her purse, she is reassured by "that dark little world, the handbag smelling of leather and cosmetics, that lay between the hostile air and her body" (*SS* 195). Once more, much closer to the time of her complete mental breakdown, Kit looks at her things: "Then she handled them absently; they were like the fascinating and mysterious objects left by a vanished civilization. . . . It did not even sadden her when she could not remember what the things meant" (*SS* 291).

The outwardness of Port and Kit's journey is reinforced by the deterioration of both their accommodations along the way and their modes of transport. Their first hotel after leaving the Mediterranean coast is shabby, but it is described as "the best hotel you'll find between here and the Congo" (*SS* 91). When they arrive at their next destination, Aïn Krorfa, they realize the full import of that statement. The Grand Hotel there features a fountain that has been turned into a garbage heap on which rest "three screaming, naked infants, their soft formless bodies troubled with bursting sores." Nearby are two dogs, pink because "their raw, aged skin" is "indecently exposed to the kisses of flies and sun" (*SS* 114). Here at Aïn Krorfa the Moresbys find weevils in their soup and clumps of fur in their stew. And here, too, Port contracts the fever that will kill him. Farther south, Port loses his passport, another sign that the structure of his identity is crumbling. As his condition worsens, they press on. There is no accommodation at all in El Ga'a because of a meningitis epidemic.

They continue traveling to a place called Sbâ, where they find lodging in a "bare little room" furnished only with a "rickety cot" (*SS* 201), the only bed in town. This is Port's final interior, but Kit's journey out is not yet done. They have arrived here in the back of an old truck—a stark contrast to the automobiles, trains, and even dilapidated buses that have brought them as far as El Ga'a. As Port lies dying, Kit wanders off on foot and is eventually picked up by a caravan. Even after she escapes from virtual slavery, she is on foot, and she is last seen running away from her rescuers into the native quarter of the coastal city where her odyssey began, lost both to reason and to civilization.

The notion of consciousness as an almost spatial structure is intimated in *The Sheltering Sky,* and this idea links the various inadequacies of architectural structure with the collapse of first Port's, then Kit's, sanity. Very early in the novel Kit reflects on "her system of omens." She feels that she can tell which days will turn out well and which will not, although her omens do sometimes play tricks with her. What is significant is her construction of this system and her belief in its existence. Her omens are really protective narrative shelters she fashions about herself to give her a sense of structure, of "insidedness," that will ward off the "doom" (*SS* 43) she feels. That doom is explicitly presented in terms of "the war between reason and atavism" (*SS* 44) within Kit. She is afraid that atavism will win the war. Her system of omens is a kind of border outpost to shore up the defense of reason. Later, extending the architectural metaphor, Kit thinks to herself that "a section of her consciousness" has "annexed" Port "as a buttress" (*SS* 83). And when she is on the brink of unreason after escaping from the Arab who kept her as his concubine, she maintains her conception of reason as an interior: "The words were coming back, and inside the wrappings of the words there would be thoughts lying there. The hot sun would shrivel them; they must be kept inside in the dark" (*SS* 302). The war, however, has been lost. Thought (reason) is "inside," but Kit is by this time so far outside that she does not even want back in.

The family structure (or "unit," as it is sometimes wishfully called) affords little sense of enclosure in *The Sheltering Sky.* Early in their journey, and somewhat later as well, the Moresbys encounter a strange, unsavory English couple. The young man,

Eric Lyle, is disreputable, and his mother is boorish and domineering. Their constant bickering is more reminiscent of a deteriorating romantic relationship than of that between a mother and son. And indeed, Port is shocked to learn from Mohammed, an Algerian he meets in Aïn Krorfa, that Eric and the woman have only pretended to be mother and son. Mohammed claims to have caught them in bed together. Yet Kit, when Port tells her Mohammed's story, insists that she has seen their passports and knows for a fact that they are what they say, although she does not seem to doubt the truth of what Mohammed purports to have witnessed. Kit speculates that Mrs. Lyle gives Eric money "on certain conditions." She suggests that "he hates all that, and is only looking for a chance to escape, and will hook up with anybody, do anything, rather than that" (*SS* 163). What those conditions are, what "that" is, is not difficult to guess. The Lyles, like the father and son in "Pages from Cold Point," are a grotesque parody of a family. The implied sexual exploitation also recalls the earlier short story, while the mother's dictatorial control over her son looks forward to Grove Soto's fear of his mother's authority in *Up Above the World.*[5]

Like the Lyle's family situation, the Moresby's marriage is a social shelter that proves insufficient, although perhaps not in so ostentatious a fashion. Port and Kit argue frequently, they are unfaithful, and they above all have difficulty being simultaneously independent and dependent, but they have genuine affection for each other and would like to salvage the marriage. From the beginning of the journey, however, they quarrel, withdraw, fail to understand. A major source of tension is Tunner, an American friend who travels with them part of the way. Kit asserts that she has "never felt completely at ease" (*SS* 20) with Tunner, and she compares him unfavorably to Port, yet she does in a moment of weakness yield to Tunner's sexual advances. She admires Port, but she is plagued by the knowledge that she "belongs" to him and is in fact dependent upon him. This problem, which might be called a domestication imbalance, is a major point of contention in many of Bowles' man/woman relationships. One partner feels too completely annexed, too thoroughly made a part of the other's interior furnishings. Most of the time Port goes his way and expects Kit to follow along sooner or later;

she is a part of his life. One night when he tries to visualize a prostitute he unsuccessfully attempted to engage, he thinks of her "in bed, without eyes to see beyond the bed . . . completely there, a prisoner" (*SS* 140). This desire for the other person to be "completely there" also informs his relationship with Kit, whether he realizes it consciously or not. The impulse that makes Kit surrender to Tunner is not unlike that which makes Van desert June in "How Many Midnights." It is an effort to break free, to furnish one's own space. Whether Van succeeds remains an unanswered question, but Kit surely does not. Having so long defined herself in terms of Port's world, she is unable to redefine herself when he dies. She is outside, with no interior of her own to substitute for his.

It is worth observing that at two of the turning points in the disintegration of their relationship, Kit's seduction by Tunner and Port's slow death, the weather outside is inclement. As Tunner enfolds Kit in his embrace, "The rain beat against the window panes" (*SS* 88), and as Port lies dying, "The wind at the window celebrated her [Kit's] dark sensation of having attained a new depth of solitude" (*SS* 218). Violent weather often functions in Bowles as a sign of the absence of any protective structure beyond those which human beings themselves piece together. The sky's uselessness as a shelter is touched on in the title of *Let It Come Down,* which is taken from *Macbeth.* When Banquo remarks, "It will be rayne tonight," the first murderer says, "Let it come down!" (III.3.15–16)—meaning not only the rain, but the knife and more broadly, the woe that pours down on Scotland and on humanity. Bowles, fascinated since childhood by this line, uses rain (and other forms of unsettled weather) to suggest things coming apart or slipping out of control. In *Up Above the World* the rain is "blinding,"[6] the woman whose name hints of protection, Mrs. Rainmantle, is murdered, and clouds lean "in a row like crooked pillars" (*UW* 16). If the world is a house, it is rapidly falling into ruin. The sky, the "roof" of the world, becomes a source of chaos, not a shield.

The meaning of the title of *The Sheltering Sky,* as it is developed in the novel, accentuates the absurdity of conceiving a cosmic shelter. Port Moresby says to his wife, "You know . . . the sky here's very strange. I often have the sensation when I look at

it that it's a solid thing up there, protecting us from what's behind." Kit asks what *is* behind, and Port replies, "Nothing, I suppose. Just darkness. Absolute night" (*SS* 101). Much later, when
she is rescued by French officialdom (but too late to save her sanity), Kit realizes the full meaning of Port's fears:

> Before her eyes was the violent blue sky—nothing else. For an end-
> less moment she looked into it. Like a great overpowering sound it
> destroyed everything in her mind, paralyzed her. Someone had once
> said to her that the sky hides the night behind it, shelters the person
> beneath from the horror that lies above. Unblinking, she fixed the
> solid emptiness, and the anguish began to move in her. At any mo-
> ment the rip can occur, the edges fly back, and the giant maw will
> be revealed. (*SS* 312)

Whereas Port—now only an anonymous "someone"—imagined
the sky as "solid" and protective, Kit fastens her attention on
"the solid emptiness," the horror beyond, and realizes how ineffectual a shelter the sky is.

Port, too, as his reason slips away, thinks of the sky, and the
diction of his thoughts forms familiar images: "He opened his
eyes, shut his eyes, saw only the thin sky stretched across to protect him. Slowly the split would occur, the sky draw back, and he
would see what he never had doubted lay behind advance upon
him with the speed of a million winds" (*SS* 233). By this time
Tunner has arrived in Sbâ and has taken Kit out for a walk.
Alone in the shabby room, Port's cry goes "on and on" (*SS* 233).
And at the precise moment Kit is telling Tunner that she loves her
husband, Port has his final vision: "A black star appears, a point
of darkness in the night sky's clarity. Point of darkness and
gateway of repose" (*SS* 235). Like Kit, Port finally thinks of the
sky more in terms of what lies behind, and although he calls it
"repose," that repose implies the dissolution of the self and the
end of humanly fashioned shelter.

In *Up Above the World* the world itself takes on an even more
menacing aspect than in *The Sheltering Sky*. There is no question
of cosmic shelter, and architectural enclosures only provide
arenas for the escalation of madness and violence. Lured into the
presumed safety of a private home, two American tourists in

Central America find it increasingly difficult to leave. The tourists, Taylor and Day Slade, become ill and have lapses of memory. All the while their host, a wealthy and charming young man named Grove Soto, is feeding them LSD and injecting them with scopolamine and morphine. He has just had his mother murdered by his friend Thorny, and he worries that the Slades, who have met her briefly en route to the city where Soto lives, might know about the crime. Eventually both Taylor and Day are killed. Soto's penthouse apartment overlooking his country's capital city is a "diamond in the sky," but it is more akin to Port Moresby's point of darkness than to the twinkling star of the nursery rhyme.[7]

Bowles himself acknowledges parallels between this melodrama and *The Sheltering Sky,* but he refers to *Up Above the World* as "an 'entertainment'" (in the manner of Graham Greene's) and says that he never considered it "a serious book like the others."[8] Indeed, there does seem to be a certain lightness about the novel, even though Bowles' "figure" or watermark is present, as indelible as ever. One reason may be that the cultural background in *Up Above the World* is just that—background. Unlike Bowles' North African novels, in which the cultural texture is an integral part of the story and has much to do with its outcome, *Up Above the World* could take place almost anywhere. The fact that Grove Soto is half Canadian and half Latin is of minor importance, and then only in terms of his own psychology. Bowles clearly does not attempt to involve whole cultures or societies in the action of this novel. Nevertheless, *Up Above the World* is not without interest, and that derives chiefly from Bowles' refusal to expand the stage of action. He focuses his attention particularly on Grove Soto, the source of danger to the traveling Slades, and in doing so not only tracks *their* drift toward exposure and destruction (as in *The Sheltering Sky*) but also suggests what can happen when the drive for security and control becomes excessive. From the Slades' point of view Soto certainly represents the dangers that lie outside the safe world they left behind. But Bowles also makes it plain (as he does, less completely, in "Pages from Cold Point" and "If I Should Open My Mouth") that not even a figure as menacing and powerful as Grove Soto is really safe.

A conversational exchange between the Slades early in their journey establishes the preoccupation with interiors that possesses many of Bowles' characters. Taylor Slade argues that they must "leave the window open" if they are to breathe in their hotel room. His wife replies that the room is "like being in a tent," but a moment later corrects herself: "'This room.' Her voice became more animated. 'It's like being outdoors'" (*UW* 26–27). Day's choice of words is important because her husband agrees to exchange places with Mrs. Rainmantle, whose own room does not lock, and it is in *this* room that Mrs. Rainmantle is murdered, by a man who climbs through the open window. This event resounds with significance. It sharpens once again the image of the window as a conduit between "safe" interiors and dangerous exteriors. It also recalls Donald's fantasy in "The Frozen Fields" of the wolf bursting through a window to kill his father. Both scenes are fictional reversals of the factual story Bowles tells about himself and his father in *Without Stopping*. Here, however, the threatening parental figure is actually killed. The hotel room's capacity to protect is obviously inadequate; and, considering Day's remark that the room is "like being outdoors," that capacity may be wholly illusory. The distinction between inside and out may itself be a fiction.

In *Up Above the World* Bowles moves quickly into the psychological dimensions of shelter, and here, too, is a link with *The Sheltering Sky*. Both novels are insistent in their projection of rationality and a stable ego as protective structures. After the drugs that Soto has administered to the Slades begin to take effect, Day finds herself "balancing at the edge of the abyss" (*UW* 119), recalling the experience of Aileen in "The Echo." Day continues to think of her loss of rationality in material and spatial terms, using words like "decentralized," "disintegration," and "decomposition" (*UW* 119). Her most vivid conceptualization of what is happening to her is explicitly architectural: "Inside, in the dark vault of her consciousness, there was an endless entry into Hell, where cities toppled and crashed upon her, and she died each time slowly, imprisoned at the bottom of the wreckage. And on the fiery horizon still more cities towered, postponing their imminent collapse until she should be within reach" (*UW* 120). In this passage as elsewhere in Bowles a close tie is forged between the idea of reason and the idea of civilization. Neither structure is very durable. The cities in Day's vision ought to promise protection; instead, their collapse only points to the caving in of the vault of consciousness itself.

Grove Soto, who has in the past been institutionalized by his mother, is keenly aware of the fragility of the house of reason. His every effort is directed toward security. Even more than John Stenham, he recoils from the thought of change. Within his penthouse/fortress, deliberately built "up above the world" in an attempt to escape the world's chaos and uncertainty, he tries to exercise absolute control. His girlfriend Luchita longs desperately to get away from him, and she in turn complicates his life because she cannot be placed under that total control. Soto's efforts in this regard recall Port Moresby's vision of the prostitute imprisoned in her bed and the Arab's locking up Kit in *The Sheltering Sky*. But for Soto everyone presents this problem; everyone, except his trusted Canadian friend Thorny, is a potential source of instability. It is therefore significant that even Thorny becomes unreliable. The novel ends with Thorny cutting his fingernails and thinking of Soto's apartment as his own house. By this time the Slades have been killed, and Thorny's knowledge of Soto's guilt is such that he will be another, even greater, source of danger. The lesson Soto cannot learn is that he can never achieve complete control; his house will never be entirely safe.

Soto thinks of the penthouse in almost metaphysical terms as a kind of heaven, with himself the godhead. He calls it "Eden" (*UW* 85), suggesting his need for a changeless, utterly predictable state. That need has its origin in a more mundane enclosure, however. One night as Soto lies in bed he has a long, complicated dream that begins with "an outsize Easter egg" (*UW* 85) through which he peers as through a window. His visual impressions keep changing, but the dominant motif is imprisonment. He sees a "glass cage" that is "one of several hundred cells," and he feels "enclosed" (*UW* 86). Looking into the egg again he seems to discern an auditorium with a screen on which appears "the face of a well-known, faded, middle-aged actress" (*UW* 87). To Soto's horror, the face on the screen turns into that of his mother, whom he characterizes as "the dark destroying presence" (*UW* 88) who had at one time had him committed. An extended interpretation of this dream is hardly necessary to catch the drift of its association of shelter, egg, womb, mother, and prison. For Soto, the image of that original shelter is not the Bachelardian nest, the primal place of security and well-being, but a jail from which he is still trying to escape. When shelter comes to be seen as prison (as it also does in *Let It Come Down*), it loses its ability to protect. Control of one's own familiar, interior space is what domestication—shelter-building—is all about. When that control slips away, one is "outside" again. Soto's suffocating feeling of being swallowed up into his *mother's* interior, subject to *her* control, is a variation on the exposure, the vulnerability, the "outsidedness," that many Bowles characters feel. Soto's experience is really only an extension into psychosis of what happens to Van in "How Many Midnights" when June takes over his apartment and his life. Van's solution is simply to disappear, surrendering that space to June. Soto counterattacks, claiming his life as his own by eliminating the intruder. In neither case can the solution be permanent.

Let It Come Down takes up more subtly than *Up Above the World* the matter of enclosure as confinement, and it also examines more thoroughly questions of solitude, relationship, and freedom. Set in Tangier when the city was still part of Morocco's International Zone, the book is in a sense a novel of intrigue, but the plotting that occurs in it extends beyond the realms of politics, espionage, and crime. Each of the major characters plots, as it were, to fashion an interior that will provide both maximum security and maximum freedom. Tangier during the days of the International Zone, a city with many identities and therefore none, is the perfect setting for a fictional exploration of the anguish involved in the construction of human identity, the most basic shelter of all. The novel's protagonist, Nelson Dyar, wants to be free and to feel alive—to be someone who counts and not just an aimless victim of circumstance. What he seeks is an identity, a sense of a selfhood and of purpose. But such a thing can be created only out of the web of human relationships that preclude absolute freedom. Dyar has let himself be "caged" in other people's patterns because he is unable to create a workable one of his own. But the solution he evolves, to isolate himself from

other people, brings not freedom but a greater sense of nothingness and of exposure to the vast nonhuman world in which we
are all outsiders.

Dyar arrives in Tangier after several unsatisfactory years as
a New York bank teller, intent on not exchanging "one cage
for another" (*LD* 22). He has been given a position in a travel
agency by an old New York acquaintance, but the agency, which
seems to do little normal business, soon proves to be a front for
currency-smuggling operations. In short order Dyar manages to
get himself involved in these dealings, to enlist in the service of
one Mme Jouvenon, a Soviet agent, and to develop a keen interest in Hadija, a Moroccan prostitute much coveted by Eunice
Goode, Tangier's most notorious lesbian. Dyar also finds himself
enmeshed in a brief flirtation with Daisy de Valverde, a wealthy
socialite and friend of Wilcox, his employer at the travel agency.
The more he becomes a part of these people's lives, the more
Dyar feels trapped. His predicament is a paradoxical one. To be
out of his "cage" he must be able to act, "to make things happen" (*LD* 153), but to do that he must know who he is—must
have an identity other than that of a victim. Like the American
protagonist described by Tony Tanner in *City of Words*, Dyar
must "establish an identity which is not a prison,"[9] but he must
also recognize that a viable identity can be constructed only socially—not in isolation. Much has been made of Bowles' debt to
Gide and to the existentialists in this novel. The dominant issue
for Dyar, however, is neither conformity versus freedom (as in
Gide) nor "fate" and responsibility (as in Camus), but the social
construction of the self. The paradox is that only by a relinquishment of the idea of total freedom can one construct the human
self—connected to other human selves—that makes limited freedom possible. Dyar never completely understands this and so
continues to drift disastrously out toward the nonhuman. Very
late in the novel, despite (if not because of) his efforts, he pain-
fully feels his exteriority: "It was the same old sensation of not
being involved, of being left out, of being beside reality rather
than in it" (*LD* 230).

Daisy de Valverde correctly diagnoses Dyar's problem at their
first meeting: "'I mean,' she said, 'that you have an empty life.
No pattern. And nothing in you to give you any purpose. Most

people can't help following some kind of design. . . . It's that that saves them'" (*LD* 34). Dyar is, again paradoxically, both outside and in. He is caged because, lacking a self-generated pattern, he must conduct the feeble movements of his life within the patterns that others impose. Or, as he himself reflects at a party later in the novel, he feels "smothered and out of place" (*LD* 118): smothered by the interiors of others, which become successive cages, and out of place because he has made no place of his own. Other characters grapple with similar problems. Thami, a young Moroccan who befriends Dyar, and whom Dyar eventually murders, is estranged from his socially prominent brothers because he has acquired a reputation as a drinker and a ne'er-do-well. His feeling of unease in the family home is central to the novel's meaning. Like Dyar, he has been unable to construct a place that is his own. His ambition to buy a boat that will, through smuggling operations, give him independent means is an important part of his effort to inject some purpose or, as Daisy says, some design into his life. Dyar later enters into this design when, after Thami has bought the boat, he hires him to take him and a valise filled with stolen bank notes to the Spanish Zone. Thami does this for money, but earlier he looks after Dyar out of a sense of responsibility. Here is where the two men differ. Dyar feels no responsibility for anything except his quest for freedom and identity; Thami from the beginning is a social creature and, as such, already has a much more developed sense of identity than Dyar. Nevertheless, in one of the closing scenes of the novel, when the two are trudging toward the hut in the Spanish Zone that will be Thami's last shelter, he feels as keenly as Dyar his outsidedness, thinking that "his soul lay in darkness, without the blessing of Allah" (*LD* 238).

Hadija, the girl sought by both Dyar and Eunice Goode, also has at least a vestigial sense of identity. She functions as best she can on the fringes of Islamic society, gleaning what benefit she can from those outsiders who control her and her city. She, too, is both caged and cast out. Her life is directed by others, and as a prostitute she cannot feel within the protective shelter of her culture even to the extent that Thami can. Yet she does have a clearly formed idea of who she is and what she can get out of life. Her function in the novel is primarily, however, to serve as a magnet bringing Dyar and Eunice—and their rather similar goals—into conflict. For Dyar she is like Port Moresby's fantasy prostitute—a thing totally under his control: "She was not a real person; it could not matter what a toy did" (*LD* 93). Dyar's earlier relations with women, before he left the United States, were similar. He and his few friends would go out on dates, but after the girls had been taken home, "they would pick up something cheap in the bar or in the street, take her to Billy Healy's room, and lay her in turn" (*LD* 21). And even in his brief, ludicrous sexual encounter with Daisy de Valverde, during which he manages to spill wine and creamed mushrooms from her dinner tray, Dyar regards his lover as a receptacle for his sperm rather than as a potential emotional tie. At this point he is intoxicated by majoun, a confection heavily laden with kif (a form of cannabis), but the affair does not differ in any significant way from those earlier ones with prostitutes. His inability to see them as "real" is symptomatic of his larger inability to form any kind of social bond—the essential step in the construction of an identity.

Eunice Goode's preoccupation with Hadija is more intense than Dyar's and far more important to her sense of self. Eunice is an outrageous creation, one of Bowles' most vivid and memorable outsiders. Her capacity for gin is surpassed only by her determination to get what she wants. A fixture in Tangier's international community, she is considered an eccentric and knows it. Her realizing her eccentricity is indistinguishable from her need to augment it; making herself an object, even of ridicule, becomes for her a method of disguise, a kind of shelter: "She told herself she did not mind being a comic character; she accepted the fact and used it to insulate herself from the too-near, ever-threatening world" (*LD* 102). Eunice is driven by the terror that haunts many of Bowles' people: the fear of exposure, of loss of control, of extinction. She therefore seeks total control over Hadija, who momentarily makes her happy: "Whenever a possibility of happiness presented itself, through it she sought to reach again that infinitely distant and tender place, her lost childhood. And in Hadija's simple laughter she divined a prospect of return" (*LD* 58).

This longing for a state of trust, comfort, and belonging—epitomized by what we all imagine childhood *should* be but seldom is—comes very close to Gaston Bachelard's conception of the primal place of repose, but in Bowles' work it is seen largely as an illusion. At one point Eunice, afraid she will lose Hadija, thinks of spiriting her away: "She began to consider places . . . where they could be alone . . . where she would have the feeling that Hadija was wholly dependent upon her" (*LD* 72). There is a certain parallel here to Dyar's relationships with women—treating them as toys rather than human beings. The similarity lies in the need for control of the situation, but it stops there. Eunice Goode, like a novelist writing a novel, knows what she is doing: "Her association with Hadija had started her off in a certain direction, which was complete ownership of the girl; and until she had the *illusion* of having achieved that, she would push ahead without looking right or left" (*LD* 155; italics added). What Eunice knows is formidable. She understands that in attempting to create a domestic situation around Hadija she is building a house; but she also knows that it is not real and that it cannot stand.

Dyar does perceive his own need for a pattern, even if he is not capable of creating one. He tells himself that he must cease being a victim (a player in other people's plots) and become a "winner." It would have to be, he reflects, "a matter of conviction, of feeling like one, of knowing you belonged to the caste, of recognizing and being sure of your genius" (*LD* 147). What he dimly intuits is the need for what I have called the creation of an interior—an imaginative (but not imaginary) space in which one can feel at home and in control. Once more, later in the novel, Daisy de Valverde puts the problem to Dyar more lucidly and forcefully than he can do himself: "You have a house. In the middle of some modest grounds, where you're used to walking about. . . . you know it's there. It's the center of your domain. Call it your objective idea about yourself" (*LD* 212). Daisy's use of the house metaphor in this scene is absolutely right, but its significance becomes twisted in Dyar's mind as he increasingly feels the influence of the majoun he has eaten. Instead of moving closer toward that house, as a place of psychic security, he begins to feel insecure and even alarmed. Thami is waiting for him outside to take him and the stolen money to the Spanish Zone; they must leave by midnight. As Daisy continues to describe the house as a place where "everything is all right," Dyar feels only his own vulnerability, "as if a gigantic hostile figure towered above him, leaning over his shoulder" (*LD* 213). Several elements coalesce in that vision: Dyar's sense of the threat to himself; the threat he himself will become when he murders Thami (leaning over him) in the little house in the Spanish Zone; and the threat of a hostile parent recounted in the artist's memoirs.

That the world outside does threaten us so relentlessly is Bowles' major theme. In *Let It Come Down* that external world is explicitly branded inhuman. The "rayne" of the epigraph includes far more than the rain that pours down on Tangier. But that simple, literal rain does serve as a constant reminder of the absolute, metaphysical exposure that makes all interiors only temporarily effective. Daisy's bedroom with its glass walls seems to Dyar "a gesture of defiance against the elements that clamored outside" (*LD* 37). On more than one occasion Dyar's frame of mind improves as the rain abates. But it is raining heavily at the beginning of the book, when Dyar arrives in Tangier, and raining again at the end, when he has lost everything. Throughout the novel windows are left open, candles blow out, doors stand ajar or will not latch. The "rayne," the vast mindless outside, cannot be kept at bay. Dyar himself glimpses the true state of affairs when Wilcox slips on dog offal and falls: "The sudden sight of a human being deprived of its dignity did not strike him as basically any more ludicrous and absurd than the constant effort required for the maintenance of that dignity, or than the state itself of being human in what seemed an undeniably non-human world" (*LD* 179). For Dyar, the effort flags, and the nonhuman world prevails.

The novel's terrible denouement catches up Daisy's image of the house as a place of psychic security and flings it in our faces. Dyar's preoccupation with the little hut's safety seems to reinforce that image, but it is the hammer and nail, which he fetches to fashion a latch, that become the murder weapon and the visible sign of his loss of humanity. When Dyar commits the act, he is again on drugs. His deliberate acceptance of both majoun and kif reveals his disinclination to make the effort required to build the house that will define and protect his humanity, or to conceive an "objective idea of himself." Even while smoking

Thami's kif, he thinks smugly of the time when "he had still been in his cage of cause and effect, the cage to which others held the keys" (*LD* 252). Yet he is here, more than ever before, "under the influence." He is more caged than ever, and more completely outside the shelter of a secure human selfhood. Just before the murder Dyar almost seems to break out of his isolation, when he says, "We . . . . would be better . . . . I think . . . . . if you can get through . . . . if you can get through . . . . Why can't anyone get through?" (*LD* 280). It is too little and far too late. By the end of the novel Dyar refers to Thami simply as "the other" (*LD* 292). When Daisy arrives to try to persuade Dyar to return and discovers the crime, she says, "I shall tell Ronny I couldn't find you" (*LD* 292). She cannot find Dyar because he has lost himself, or perhaps more accurately, he has found an unutterable strangeness within himself. Kif, as Daisy says of majoun earlier in the novel, can lead to a fearsome discovery: "You find absolutely new places inside yourself, places you feel simply couldn't be a part of you, and yet there they are" (*LD* 213). This is what happens to Dyar. There can be no shelter from the "other" because there can be no distinction from it. Even the shelter of a familiar selfhood appears an illusion. As darkness falls, Dyar has relinquished the marginal existence as a human being that he once possessed. The imperative mood of the novel's title seems at this point a cruel, ironic joke on all our feeble attempts at finding shelter: *Let It Come Down*. As if we had any choice.

3. Going Outside

I

PAUL BOWLES' EXTENSIVE TRAVELS and self-imposed exile have provided him with an intimate experiential model for his fictional explorations of the world outside. As a small child Bowles passed the time by inventing place-names, fictional places, even a fictional "planet with landmasses and seas" (*WS* 27). His urge to strike out into uncharted territory soon began to find other outlets, such as occasional family visits to a friend's summer house on Long Island: "For me there were sandy paths through the wilderness of beach plum and scrub oak. The excitement inherent in exploring an unknown terrain was big enough to keep me fully occupied" (*WS* 52). Moving about in foreign cultures, learning how to live in them, has been for Bowles a kind of defiance of the unknown exterior. He has always sought the unfamiliar, a point he stresses in the first sentence of *Their Heads Are Green and Their Hands Are Blue:* "Each time I go to a place I have not seen before, I hope it will be as different as possible from the places I already know."[1] Bowles' travel writings, such as the essays in *Their Heads Are Green*, are attempts at exploration, explanation, making cultural unknowns more familiar. One of the most successful of these is "A Man Must Not Be Very Moslem," in which Bowles' own worldly, western point of view alternates with the insights and opinions of Abdeslam, a young Moroccan he once took with him to Turkey. That dual perspective is essentially the same exploratory technique that Bowles employs with great effect in *The Spider's House*. Exploration has determined to a large degree the patterns of Bowles' life, and exploration is perhaps the central shaping force within his fiction.

Graham Greene, reflecting on the human impulse to step into the unknown, invests it with a psychological significance. Our fear of the outside, Greene says, is of "a force exerted on a door

... and pressed against the windows."[2] It is that which might intrude on the inside. Greene explains his own travels through the remotest regions of Liberia in terms of this lingering fear and the desire to confront and overcome it. For him, the ultimate symbol of that outside force, the utterly alien, has always been old Gagool, the witch in H. Rider Haggard's *King Solomon's Mines*. Haggard's heroes did not seem real to Greene, he recalls, but "Gagool I could recognize—didn't she wait for me in dreams every night, in the passage by the linen cupboard, near the nursery door?" And so, as if to encounter and tame Gagool, Greene went to West Africa "to the same region of the imagination—the region of uncertainty, of not knowing the way about."[3] John Stenham's wanderings outside the walls of Fez in *The Spider's House*, through areas whose "beauty existed for him only to the degree that he was conscious of their outsidedness" (*SH* 166), are motivated by a similar need. Domestication can be attempted, as I have indicated earlier, either by exclusion of the alien or by enclosure and transformation of it. Going outside, extending the area of psychic (or cultural) "safety," is the heart of exploration.

Cultural interpenetration can be seen in Bowles both as a central area of thematic concern—a "subject"—and as a paradigm for all our attempts to annex the strange. Bowles' work is not unique in this regard. There is a century-old literary tradition, beginning in earnest with the publication of *King Solomon's Mines* in 1885, in which domestication of the alien, in thematic and structural terms, is paramount: the tradition of the imperialist romance[4] and related fictional forms. Unlike Graham Greene, Bowles has not been influenced directly by Rider Haggard, but he falls into a line of later writers who invert Haggard's cozy colonial formulas. The conjunction of first and third worlds is central to Bowles' work, and the strangeness, the otherness, of alien cultures appears at the core of his fiction as frequently as it does in the imperialist romance. This now outmoded type of adventure tale, with its urgently communicated need to domesticate, to bring what is extrinsic and unfamiliar into the house of empire, confronts on its deepest levels (although from a radically different perspective) the same issues of shelter and exposure that most concern Bowles.

The reason for the sudden popularity of the imperialist romance in the mid-1880's is not difficult to guess. In its most pristine form, it chronicles the adventures of European explorers who travel into previously uncharted territory and establish their benevolent influence among the primitive (dark-skinned) natives. The late Victorians must have found in this basic plot an immensely flattering image of their own imperial situation. Other common structural elements of the genre tend to reflect related cultural attitudes.[5] For instance, in many imperialist romances the explorers discover the ruins of an ancient white civilization—proof positive that even in the distant past something approximating a colonial condition prevailed. Seen in this light, European penetration merely constitutes restoration of the old (and correct) order, in which various "Dark Continents" were part of a comfortably familiar white domain, often conceived as having values and customs akin to those of nineteenth-century Britain. What Bowles' characters usually discover, on the other hand, is an alien culture that refuses to be domesticated.

Natives encountered by the adventurers in the imperialist romance are typically divided into two competing factions or warring tribes—one hostile, the other amenable to westernization. Sometimes animals are placed in the structural position of the hostile native faction, clearly indicating the imperialists' tendency to reserve human qualities to themselves. The late Victorians were extraordinarily preoccupied with the indistinctness of the borders between the savage and the civilized, the animal and the human. The potential nonhuman within was greatly feared, so it was objectified and externalized as a way of forcing it out the door. Edward Said, in *Orientalism*, treats this attitude primarily as a European phenomenon (or more accurately, neurosis): ". . . a white middle-class Westerner believes it is his human prerogative not only to manage the nonwhite world but also to own it, just because by definition 'it' is not quite as human as 'we' are." But surely the inclination to construct a human order (Peter Berger's *nomos*, if you will) and to deny human value and purpose to that which lies outside it, must be seen in the larger framework of meaning-creation and order-construction as a protective process that is inherently transcultural. Said himself admits that "domestications of the exotic take place between all cultures . . . and between all men."[6] The intensity of the fear of the savage or nonhuman in the late nineteenth century was probably fueled by a combination of the debate over Darwin and a growing sense of the precariousness of empire. The imperialist romance exhibits the need for such domestication as forthrightly as it can be exhibited. The "good" (more civilized, more human) native faction wins the struggle, but only with the active intervention of the European visitors. The whites, having established their kind of order, depart with an immense feeling of satisfaction, having illuminated the darkness and brought some of the alien exterior into the house of European civilization. Just how far Bowles departs from this pattern (while at the same time confronting some of the same issues), will be seen when we look at stories like "Pastor Dowe at Tacaté."

The pervasiveness and popularity of the imperialist romance over several decades cannot be explained solely by the impact of a single writer, however widely read his works might have been. The full explanation lies in a combination of historical circumstance (the approaching twilight of empire) and collective psychology (the urge, in the face of innumerable "new" lands and cultures, to feel the world to be a safe, familiar place). This need also explains why the imperialist romance is so end-centered. In all narratives that involve a journey out, as many of Paul Bowles' do, the implicit (though not always the actual) ending is the return home. In the imperialist romance, going out generates the action and coming home makes the action meaningful. Coming home is crucial, even when it is not explicitly presented. Through the domestication of the alien, the establishment of order, and the imposition of European values, the outside world is to some extent made a part of home. In this way the story is twice closed. The domesticating mission is accomplished, *and* the heroes are returned to their inmost sanctuaries of hearth and home, kith and kin. The customary first-person narrative points to such an ending by assuring readers that the hero has long since safely arrived home. His bold deeds and outward thrusts are "contained" within the shelter of a narrated past even as the novel begins. As time went on and empire waned, the imperialist romance gradually degenerated into increasingly implausible fantasy-adventures set on lost continents, in the center of the earth, and eventually on other planets. What is more interesting, and more pertinent to Bowles, is that the genre's underlying values began to be challenged, and its patterns deliberately violated, as early as the 1890's by saboteurs like Olive Schreiner, H. G. Wells, and particularly Joseph Conrad.

It is possible to place the plot of *Lord Jim* into such a Procrustean bed as to make the novel appear to be a conventional imperialist romance. A young Englishman, intent upon proving himself, has a series of high adventures in the East Indies. He encounters hostile and friendly natives. In alliance with Doramin and his son, who is said to have a European mind, Jim defeats the evil Sherif Ali and manages to keep the equally unsavory Rajah Allang under control. A new civilized order is established. One cannot help noticing that this new order involves the subordination of Moslem authority to that of a European (Christian) leader. Conrad seems here to displace quite neatly two "oriental" cultures. "Rajah" is a title that derives from the Sanskrit language of Hindu India; and a sherif is a descendant of the Prophet Mohammed. When Marlow last sees Jim, things appear (for Jim) to be steadily improving. But the novel does not conveniently "tie up" at that point, with Jim well on his way to making Patusan another outpost of progress. And indeed, it is evident how many elements (ranging from Jim's relatively unprepossessing height to his major flaw) must be suppressed to make even the novel's first half conform to the lineaments of the imperialist romance. Yet the similarities make the significance of the differences all the more striking.

I have mentioned that coming home, both in the sense of domesticating the alien and in the sense of getting the hero back safely to his point of origin, is the dominant idea in the imperialist romance—an idea that can be traced as far back as the genre's prototype, *Robinson Crusoe.* This is also the most important point of intersection between the imperialist romance and the fiction of Paul Bowles. Port Moresby is certainly not alone among Bowles' characters in finding "it difficult to tell, among the many places he had lived, precisely where it was he had felt most at home" (*SS* 14). But it was Conrad who first grasped the consequence of the issue and brought it into the light of day, creating in the process a new literary tradition. Jim's own home is graphically described in the novel's first chapter, and the image

is subsequently vitalized by a letter from his father. Conrad
understood explicitly what Haggard merely intuited: that home
is much more than a geographical entity. It is the sense of repose
to which all human beings, as Bachelard says, must periodically
return, even if its protection is only illusory. Early in *Lord Jim,*
before Marlow's narration begins, the general narrator offers a
glimpse of the shelter Jim has constructed for himself: "Jim on
the bridge was penetrated by the great certitude of unbounded
safety and peace that could be read on the silent aspect of nature
like the certitude of fostering love upon the placid tenderness of a
mother's face."[7] That shelter collapses when the accident occurs,
but the need for it remains. Jim's efforts to construct a domicile,
a place to feel at home, in Patusan should come as no surprise.
Halfway through the novel Marlow waxes eloquent (*he* calls it
sentimental) about going back "to that home distant enough for
all its hearthstones to be like one hearthstone" (*LJ* 159). The
speech takes on a distinctly graver tone when Marlow observes,
"He would never go home now. Not he. Never" (*LJ* 160).

Conrad's two most radical departures from the imperialist romance pattern relate directly to a shift in fundamental values and
assumptions, and as such they prepare the way for later writers
like Paul Bowles. One departure is that the hero does not go
home. The other is that he cannot make a home where he is; he
cannot domesticate the alien. "Leave!" Jim exclaims. "For where?
What for?" (*LJ* 178). Patusan is the home he has. But like his
sense of well-being at the beginning of the novel, this shelter is
temporary. The failure to create a secure domicile out of the alien
darkness can be read in purely political (i.e., anti-imperialistic)
terms. Conrad's repeated insistence on the utter inconceivability
of taking Jim (or, for that matter, Kurtz) back home to Europe,
however, gives these configurations deeper and more frightening
meaning. What was once "home" for Jim finally becomes simply
"out there" (*LJ* 239). The distinctions between inside and outside, shelter and exposure, "us" and "them," are blurred. Patusan, the place of refuge and reconstruction, is Patna and us;
Jim is one of us. And at the end of the novel "Gentleman" Brown
comes from "out there" and identifies himself with Jim, as if to
say not only that no one is good enough, but that no humanly
fashioned "home" is safe enough.

Shlomith Rimmon-Kenan, drawing on both Jonathan Culler
and Menakhem Perry, discusses the conventions of genre as es-
tablishing "a kind of contract between the text and the reader, so
that some expectations are rendered plausible, others ruled out,
and elements which would seem strange in another context are
made intelligible within the genre." As we read, we construct
"models of coherence" that can be derived from either experience or literary and cultural conventions.[8] Insofar as the imperialist romance is concerned, the primary literary convention contributing to intelligibility was the much older convention of the
romance quest. But even more important were political and psychological factors. The imperialist romance was the canonical
novelistic form for the imaging of Europe's nineteenth-century
encounter with alien cultures, and, as such, it was a literary
manifestation of a deeply felt, and probably universal, human
need to be assured that the shelters of order, stability, and rationality could be maintained and even extended. Conrad's fiction
called this assurance into question and in doing so created a new
context in which domestication and alienation could be explored
by later writers, ranging from E. M. Forster and George Orwell
to Graham Greene, V. S. Naipaul, Peter Matthiessen, and Paul
Bowles. The literature of exploration and cultural interaction has
changed over the past century as the alien and the outside have
come to seem closer, more a part of our lives. What Bowles has
done is to marshal and direct his own personal imaginative experience in such a way as to make himself the most eloquent contemporary analyst of the terror that, in Greene's words, lies
"pressed against the windows."[9]

II

The closeness of the alien and its stubborn refusal to be domesticated can be clearly seen in an early Bowles story, "Pastor Dowe
at Tacaté," that neatly inverts the imperialist romance formula.
Pastor Dowe is a missionary struggling to bring "the truth" to an
isolated Indian village in South America. What an imperialist ro-
mancer would make of this situation is not difficult to imagine.
Conversions to Christianity would compete with discovery of a
lost treasure (of no use to the happy primitives) to make Pastor

Dowe's material triumph as glittering as his spiritual one. But this is not what happens. Instead, an accumulation of small defeats points to the failure of the mission: Dowe begins to feel "wholly alone in this distant place" (CS 140); the people refuse to listen to Dowe's sermons unless he punctuates them with music played on an old phonograph—the 1928 show tune, "Crazy Rhythm"; and two natives take the pastor on a downriver excursion to the shrine of a pagan god, Metzabok, during which Dowe realizes just how intractable the alien is. They enter a region (which becomes a figure for the whole world) that seems "outside God's jurisdiction," and he thinks, "Now it is done. I have passed over into the other land" (CS 148–149). When he returns to the comparative safety of the village to perform his weekly ceremony, a seven-year-old girl lets her pet alligator (which the pastor regards as vaguely obscene) slip out of her arms and run amok through the congregation. Shortly after this episode the girl's father, Nicolás, offers her to Dowe as a wife, and Mateo, Dowe's servant, urges him to accept. Enraged, frustrated, and demoralized, Dowe shouts, "'You don't understand anything! . . . I can't talk to you! I don't want to talk to you! Go out and leave me alone" (CS 154). Not long afterward the pastor decides to abandon his flock. Packing his Bible, toothbrush, and medicine—the little props supporting his sense of the domestic—he wanders off into the jungle, his mission spectacularly unaccomplished.

The missionary enterprise is the most thorough form of imperialism because it undertakes to rip up and replace the very roots of a culture—a people's understanding of who they are and how they relate to the rest of the universe. From the outset Pastor Dowe is only half aware of the magnitude of his task. Not comprehending the Indians' cosmology, he substitutes the name of their god Hachakyum for that of the Judeo-Christian God in his sermons, only to be told that the Indians do not believe in a single creator. "Hachakyum did not make everyone," Nicolás explains. "He did not make you. He did not make guns or Don Jesucristo" (CS 139). From the Indians' point of view, he, his civilization, his savior—"all the things that do not belong here" (CS 139)—were created by the god called Metzabok. When Dowe later finds himself unwittingly praying at a place that turns out to be Metzabok's shrine, he has indeed "passed over into the other land." He has gone so far into the alien that his sense of who *he* is has been severely undermined. On the way back from the river expedition Dowe stops at Nicolás' hut, where the Indian proudly displays his most prized possessions: "some sample-sized squares of printed cloth, an old vial of quinine tablets, a torn strip of newspaper, and four copper coins" (*CS* 150). These treasures are the detritus of western culture. Their importance lies in the fact that they have been appropriated by Nicolás and made into something else. In the same way an Indian woman retrieves Dowe's discarded glasses case and begins to work it into something of use to her. Perhaps Dowe fears that his life will become like these objects—no longer alien to the Indians but a part of their immediate reality. When he walks away from Tacaté he saves himself from such a fate, but he also implicitly admits that he has failed to bring the Indians into *his* world. Irving Caesar's absurdly inappropriate, yet curiously pertinent, lyrics must echo in his mind: "Crazy rhythm, here's a doorway / I'll go my way, you'll go your way / Crazy rhythm, from now on we're through."

Among the many other Bowles stories following this general plan, one of the most interesting and powerful is "A Distant Episode," in which a linguist visiting a remote region in North Africa finds that the friend he has expected to see is dead. The professor has as clearly defined a purpose for his journey as any hero in H. Rider Haggard. He means to study local dialects and, if possible, acquire a small leather box made from a camel's udder to add to his collection. His overnight bags are filled with "maps, sun lotions, and medicines" (*CS* 39)—important sources of psychic support in Bowles' travel stories. Those items are conduits to the traveler's home culture and reassurances that he can extend the boundaries of that home. But the purposefulness of the quest, as well as its chances for success, is undercut immediately, and not only by the news of the friend's death. The café where the professor searches for his friend has a back room that hangs "hazardously out above the river" (*CS* 40). A surly stranger takes him out of the village (the beginning of the second of three journeys out) to find one of the boxes. All along the way danger signals multiply. The native tells the professor that "no one" in this area knows him. The road winds "downward." There are "bad dogs" and "the odor of human excrement" (*CS* 41). Before leaving the linguist in the dark at the edge of a pit, the native guide urges him to descend into it if he wants a camel's-udder box.

As the story's plot unfolds, it reveals itself as a process of unlearning rather than of learning, of increasing disorder and strangeness rather than of gathering control and familiarity. The professor, after having listened for a while to the orderly, patterned music of a flute coming "from somewhere down below" now hears "only the wind going by his ears" (*CS* 42). As he begins his descent into the pit, he reflects: "Only the wind was left behind, above, to wander among the trees, to blow through the dusty streets of Aïn Tadouirt, into the hall of the Grand Hotel Saharien, and under the door of his little room" (*CS* 43). Clearly at this point in the story the world outside encroaches on "safe" interiors. The professor, explicitly acknowledging this, thinks of his descent as an "irrational thing" (*CS* 44). When first dogs, then men, attack him, his efforts to impose an acceptable, civilized order on an unacceptably horrific and chaotic experience break down:

> When the Professor opened his mouth to breathe, the man swiftly seized his tongue and pulled on it with all his might. The Professor was gagging and catching his breath; he did not see what was happening. He could not distinguish the pain of the brutal yanking from that of the sharp knife. Then there was an endless choking and spitting that went on automatically, as though he were scarcely a part of it. The word "operation" kept going through his mind; it calmed his terror somewhat as he sank back into darkness. (*CS* 45)

Sinking back into darkness is what this story is largely about. The professor is dumped into a sack and transported across the desert to dance mindlessly for the entertainment of women and children. Scarcely more than an animal at this point, his days are passed in eating, defecating, and sleeping with the camels.

During the months that follow, the professor experiences only a partial return to consciousness and humanity. Shortly after he does, he finds himself locked in a house by a man who has recently bought him from his original captors. His ties to reason gone, he retains only enough wit to escape. Ripping apart the house and its furnishings, breaking down the door, he runs outside toward the setting sun. Here at the end of the story begins the third and final journey out, this one representing the final, irrevocable triumph of the outside and the utter collapse of human order.

Language is first thought by the professor to be an aspect of culture that can be studied and thereby intellectually enclosed. As such, it becomes for him a medium for cultural penetration. The linguist/scholar is a type of explorer who wishes to "know" a people through its language and in so doing to make the strange less strange. His unspoken purpose is hence actually quite close to that of Allan Quatermain in *King Solomon's Mines*. But there are intimations from the story's first page that language cannot adequately fulfill this function. A chauffeur tells the professor when he first arrives in the village, "Keep on going south. . . . You'll find some languages you never heard of before" (*CS* 39), suggesting, if only faintly, that there might be regions outside the realm of understanding, beyond the reach of domestication. When he is being taken to the pit by the native guide, the professor asks if he will be working at the café the next day, and the guide replies, "That is impossible to say" (*CS* 41). Here and throughout the story communication is difficult and language is presented as an unstable repository for determinate truth. After the professor is set upon, he tries to reason with his attackers, but he cannot make the words come. The gruesome tongue-cutting that ensues, and the professor's inarticulate bellowing at the end of the story, only re-emphasize the ultimate ineffectuality of language. We must be reminded here of the dust blowing into the mouth of the helpless Moungari in "The Delicate Prey." Few of Bowles' stories (and none of his novels) end in the midst of conversation. Indeed, it is remarkable how many conclude like "A Distant Episode," with a commanding silence, a cessation of talking, with language itself standing as the last structure thrown up by the human in defense against the grim other.

A novel that Bowles never finished, and which exists only in unpublished manuscript fragments, baldly displays how completely Bowles' journeys out fail to achieve their goals. As the narrative opens, a bored American schoolteacher is in correspondence with a wealthy Latin American landowner whom she eventually marries. Her quest, like that of Dyar in *Let It Come Down*, is motivated by a distinct feeling of discomfort at home and a sense that her life lacks direction. In an early scene her mind wanders from her teaching duties as she gazes out a classroom window. She is clearly not at home in this place. Here as elsewhere in Bowles the window is a primary figure for an imagined border between the safe and the strange. She crosses over that border, ultimately making her way to the town nearest her fiancé's estate. Even then she considers not going through with this marriage to a man she has never met, but he sends a servant to fetch her, and "she goes, without knowing why." Scenes following the marriage, according to Bowles' notes, are intended to reveal increasing "incompatibility of husband and wife." [10]

Beyond this point the novel is sketched out cryptically but vividly to its conclusion. The woman becomes pregnant by a native gardener and gives birth to a son, which her husband thinks belongs to him. When the husband dies, the gardener tries to assert his rights, but the woman contrives to have him arrested and sent away. As the years pass, the boy grows up (the envy of local mothers because of his light skin), and the house gradually falls into ruin. At last the woman is forced to move out completely and into the gardener's vacated hut. Her "going native" in this way in a sense constitutes her second expatriation and stands as a blunt reminder of how completely her foray into alien territory has failed. She has neither found a sense of direction nor made for herself in the outside world a home that is any more suitable than the one she left behind. Eventually she is reduced to telling the fortunes of native women and selling her son's sexual services to them. When he goes away she replaces him with a halfwit she finds in a nearby town and spends the rest of her years in fear that the gardener will return and discover the deception. Lawrence Stewart summarizes the final stages of the novel in this way: "The gardener is released from prison and returns. Thinking the half-wit is his son grown up, he again tries to take control of the property, and this time the mother incites the 'son' to kill him" (*PB* 154–155). Bowles' notes do spell out these events, but with the preface, "She spins fantasy," which leads me to believe that the gardener was never intended actually to come back. In either case it is difficult to ascertain from fewer than twenty pages of fragmentary outline how forceful a novel this might have been. Bowles abandoned it because it was "too melodramatic," though some of its elements found their way into *Up Above the World*.[11] But it is instructive sometimes to examine a blueprint because the essential lines are usually there. In this instance they are the outward journey, the implicit desire to extend one's sphere of familiarity or to replace an uncomfortable pattern with a familiar one, the search for purpose or meaning, and the drift into a greater and greater condition of exposure until all is lost. Order is not imposed; the very idea of purpose is forgotten; and a "broken ceiling" at the end of the fragment spirals back to the window image in the first scene in a final erasure of the line between inside and out. Alien culture becomes a metaphor for all that lies beyond our ken, and that, finally, may be all there is.

"At Paso Rojo" is a modification of the Bowles journey in that the expedition is to a place already "known"; but for that very reason it highlights the notion that the unknowable is everywhere. The story also cuts very close to the bone on the question of difference between "whites" and "natives," and that question expands to the larger one of the distinction between familiar self and alien other. As Conrad does in *Heart of Darkness* (and as H. Rider Haggard emphatically does *not* do), Bowles blurs these distinctions, suggesting that the wild and strange cling closely to the familiar. The idea that the wild can be "in the house," as we have already seen, vitalizes such stories as "Pages from Cold Point," "The Frozen Fields," and "The Echo." Here it assumes added significance because it is set in the framework of a journey of exploration and domestication. In "At Paso Rojo" two sisters, Lucha and Chalía, "leave the city and go down to Paso Rojo for a few weeks" (*CS* 121). There, in the interior of their country, lies their brother Federico's ranch. Considering the ranch primitive and barbarous, the sisters' unspoken goal is to civilize it to some extent—primarily by impressing on Federico the importance of clear distinctions between themselves and native servants. The ranch's status as a foreign, "outside" place is stressed by frequent references to the insects, night birds, and monkeys whose presence frightens and annoys the travelers from the city.

The more eccentric sister, Chalía, one day goes out for a ride with Federico and an Indian hired hand named Roberto. When Roberto gently rebuffs her rather blunt sexual advances, she re-

solves to punish him. That evening she pulls him aside and gives
him a large amount of money she has stolen from her brother.
Much later in the night she goes out for a walk, finds Roberto
lying drunk in the road, and kicks him over a small cliff. The conflict with the Indian points up a difference between Bowles' work
and the imperialist romance that goes to the heart of the matter
of domestication. As in many novels by Rider Haggard and his
imitators, natives are here identified with animals, making them
completely alien. Lucha calls them "animals with speech" (*CS*
121), and Chalía notices "a strange animal sound" (*CS* 133)
when she kicks Roberto over the embankment. But in the imperialist romance some of those animals are successfully "tamed";
some natives are brought "inside the house" of European civilization. In "At Paso Rojo" the reverse occurs. The native Roberto is
already more civilized, and certainly more civil, than the lady
from the city. She, however, displays the "wild" characteristics
that she considers his natural inheritance. The sisters consistently
attempt to deny the unfamiliar by casting it far outside. What
they fail to understand is how capable of atavistic violence they
themselves may be. Chalía's attack on Roberto, while specifically
motivated by an assumed sexual affront, also has a deeper meaning. Several times in Bowles a white person harms a native. In
"The Echo" Aileen strikes a youth with a stone; in "The Hours
after Noon" Monsieur Royer, a Frenchman, strikes a Moroccan
child "a savage blow in the face" (*CS* 223); the photographer in
"Tapiama" kicks a mulatto girl "full in the breast" (*CS* 283); in
the unwritten novel the schoolteacher has the gardener, the father
of her child, sent to jail; in *Let It Come Down* Nelson Dyar drives
a nail through Thami's ear. An intense, barely repressed sexual
frustration lies behind most of these incidents. The white characters (and I would include here even Dyar, whose relationship to
Thami is more than a little homoerotic) are simultaneously re-
pelled by the otherness of the natives and sexually attracted to it.
Sexual conquest is a primary means of domestication in human
relations, but when repulsion and fear become dominant, as they
so often do in Bowles, the result is more usually an act of violence
than of love. The alien is overcome by annihilating it—by simply
destroying that which lies "outside." In most cases the strategy

ends in failure, however, with the protagonist left more outside than ever, having abandoned all the protective, "civilized" forms of conduct.

Chalía dimly recognizes the psychological process she is undergoing. After her rejection by Roberto, she reflects: "She, being inside herself, existed merely as herself and not as a part of anything else. People, animals, flowers and stones were objects, and they all belonged to the world outside." Perhaps more explicitly than anywhere else in Bowles, human identity is defined by Chalía as the construction of an interior, a safe place that will keep the outside out. But even here, she feels "that almost all of her had slipped out of the inside world, that only a tiny part of her was still she" (*CS* 129). She imagines that she retains this small, safe interior, but at the end of the story, when her corruption is complete, she admits to herself that she has begun to "enjoy" life at Paso Rojo. Far from annexing the world outside, she has become part of it.

III

The Sheltering Sky may well be Bowles' most extended treatment of the failure of the journey out, and it is certainly one of his most striking accounts of the dangers inherent in going "too far." The Moresbys' travels deep into the Sahara are not directed toward so clear a goal as Pastor Dowe's desire to convert the heathen, but they do conceive of their journey as an "expedition . . . into the unknown" (*SS* 105), and Kit refers to it facetiously as "our great trek" (*SS* 56), recalling an earlier, more successful domesticating mission. Port Moresby thinks of himself as a traveler, not a tourist, and the distinction is important to him. Tourism is farther removed from exploration and hence from those psychic satisfactions that accrue from the annexation of the alien into one's "own" territory.[12] Yet Port admits, "I always imagine that somehow I'll be able to penetrate to the interior of somewhere. Usually I get just about to the suburbs and get lost" (*SS* 167). This is, of course, literally what has happened to Port very early in the novel, and it can be seen as a figure for what happens to him at the end.

If the Moresbys' subliminal goal is to gather into their region of familiarity the great outside, a more immediate aim is to save their faltering marriage. Port tells himself that the "desire to strengthen the sentimental bonds between them" (*SS* 105) is what he must have had "subconsciously" in mind when they left New York. Like a number of other couples in Bowles, Port and Kit have become strangers to one another; their need to re-create "the sentimental bonds between them," to fashion a space where both can feel familiar together (without either being dominated or "colonized" by the other), originates from the same psychic source as the urge to travel in foreign lands. Both involve an obsessive longing to roll back the borders of the strange, to expand the imagined area of interiority. On the most superficial level this phenomenon assumes the form of escape, for the novel takes place after World War II, and the Moresbys are also in flight from the homogenization of postwar technological society. In seeking to domesticate the foreign, they implicitly recognize that they are already "outside." Their own home culture has lost its meaning, ceased to fulfill the function of home.

As the Moresbys move more and more deeply into the desert, it becomes increasingly evident that their goals will not be realized. Rather than making this alien place their own, they are gradually defeated by it. Each town they visit seems stranger, more foreign, more forbidding, until their own foreignness appears to them in its totality. They are out of place in the world. A passage early in the novel presages this revelation. Port looks around him at the hotel bar in Oran, where the journey begins, and reflects on "the sadness inherent in all deracinated things" (*SS* 57). He speculates that "happiness" might be found farther into Africa, "but not here in this sad colonial room where each invocation of Europe was merely one more squalid touch, one more visible proof of isolation" (*SS* 57–58). The signs of an earlier attempt at domestication are sad because they are so clearly the evidence of its failure, like the decaying machinery and broken-down railway car in *Heart of Darkness*. The sadness makes Port all the more uneasy because he has felt it the day before, upon awakening: "He was somewhere, he had come back through vast regions from nowhere; there was the certitude of an infinite sadness at the core of his consciousness, but the sadness was reassuring, because it alone was familiar" (*SS* 11). Bowles seems to be saying here, though with almost invisible subtlety, that the sadness of deracination underlies all else, that all of us are ineluctably outside, which is to say "nowhere."

There is a good deal of preoccupation in *The Sheltering Sky* with the idea of going too far. The shelter (whether architectural, societal, or psychological) that Bowles' characters frequently abandon in their journeys out may be illusory, but they usually discover that it is all they have. Penetrating to the suburbs and getting lost is precisely what Port does in Oran, although in this case he does manage to get back. Kit, similarly, wanders off during a train ride with Tunner, and finds herself in a surrealistically grotesque scene in one of the "native" cars. But she, too, returns. Much later in the novel, when she has disappeared into the desert, Tunner thinks of the incident as a nightmare, telling himself that she will reappear as she did on the train. She does reappear, of course, but only briefly before her final disappearance at the end of the novel, and the telegram she tries to send precisely describes what has happened to her: "CANNOT GET BACK" (*SS* 304). Port and Kit wander too far from whatever "home" means to them and are lost, swallowed up by the immense, indifferent outside.

Geographical exploration is frequently associated with mental wandering in Bowles' work. The pattern repeats itself many times. The photographer in "Tapiama" drinks too much *cumbiamba* in a faraway Latin American outpost and finds that he cannot free himself "from the irrational ideas boiling up in his head" (*CS* 290). The professor in "A Distant Episode" loses all sense of who and what he is during his travels. And in both *Up Above the World* and *Let It Come Down* the breakdown of rationality parallels the journey out. In *The Sheltering Sky* Port's delirium and Kit's derangement have different causes, but they are alike in their effects. Like other Bowles characters in similar situations they suffer a wrenching removal from a reality they conceive of as a familiar place. Kit's "things," which she arranges and admires on several occasions, are totems of order and meaning as well as artifacts of western civilization. Loss of that order implies an alienation more complete than any geographical one could be. Port from the beginning of the novel thinks of his identity as "here"—a place where he feels safe. Waking up is a coming back from oblivion. And Kit, talking to Tunner on the train, makes "a great effort to be present" (*SS* 78)—to keep from wandering off mentally. When Port becomes ill, he says to her, "I don't know whether I'll come back" (*SS* 210). A bit later he says, "I've been trying to get back" (*SS* 215). But in the end the effort is too much for him: "Sometimes I'm not here, and I don't like that. Because then I'm far away and all alone. No one could ever get there. It's too far. And there I'm alone" (*SS* 216). "Here" in Bowles is a place where one can at least imagine an identity and a vestigial sense of safety. "There" is everything beyond the window, and that exterior is beyond annexation.

The literal and metaphorical aspects of the journey out are joined very effectively in "Here to Learn," where, as in *The Sheltering Sky*, the traditional paradigm of domestication is replaced by that of going too far. Port and Kit not only fail to bring the alien world in; they also fail to return to the world from which they came—a world, moreover, that was already foreign to them. In this important sense Bowles' work is the antithesis of the end-centered imperialist romance. "Here to Learn," the longest tale in *Midnight Mass*, gives the usual Bowles pattern still another twist. Instead of recounting a foray into the third world by a westerner, the story focuses on a Moroccan girl's odyssey from her village in the Rif to the wilds of Los Angeles. But the basic Bowles plot is still there: the journey into the unknown, the movement outside the great window that divides the safe from the strange.

Malika's travels in "Here to Learn" take her into areas that seem increasingly foreign. In this respect her journey does not differ markedly from those of the Moresbys, Pastor Dowe, the linguist in "A Distant Episode," the schoolteacher in the unfinished novel, and many other Bowles characters who move from the west into the "primitive" world. The fact that Malika's heart of darkness lies in the opposite direction unmistakably establishes that the alien, at least in Bowles, cannot be seen in purely political, cultural, or historical terms. Cultural contrast is central to the story's meaning, however, and the incongruities that arise out of Malika's accelerating sense of strangeness contribute greatly to its humor. Still, the impression left by "Here to Learn" is that the world is intrinsically and universally alien, and that the strange as well as the safe is largely a state of mind.

The first stage of Malika's journey begins when she accepts a ride with a "Nazarene" named Tim. She has had trouble with her mother at home and is therefore more receptive than she might otherwise have been to this kind of adventure. Feeling that she had made "an irrevocable choice" (*MM* 51), Malika goes with Tim to his apartment in Tangier and lives with him there. When he is called to London on business, he leaves her in the care of two homosexual friends. During his absence a third homosexual, Tony, delighted with Malika, spirits her off, first to Madrid, then to Paris. Malika is entranced with the western clothes her friends buy her and is eager to learn more about western languages and culture because her father told her long before that "Allah has sent us here to learn" (*MM* 43). Eventually she meets and marries a wealthy American who takes her to his home in Los Angeles. After his death in an automobile crash, Malika returns to her village in Morocco to give her mother money but finds that her mother has died and the house has been bulldozed.

From the outset Malika has been preoccupied with the question of safety. When her mother, very early in the story, tells her to go to the market on the main highway to sell a hen, she asks permission to wear a *haik* to conceal her great beauty from the soldiers. Her mother refuses, and the lesson Malika learns is a brutal one. A soldier grabs her, bruising her arm. Her mother sees the bruise, slaps her, and calls her a "young bitch" (*MM* 46). Much later, at her husband Tex's tree-shaded house in Los Angeles, she is relieved that the windows have bars and the door has heavy bolts, but she still worries about how safe the house can be. She does not feel "at ease" sitting on the sun-deck "with nothing between her and the dark forest" (*MM* 80). Paradoxically, she feels most exposed in Los Angeles, where she is under the protection of a loving husband. This is because she sees the shelter of his affection as only temporary, and she has traveled farther from her sphere of familiarity than ever before: "She had the impression that in America everyone was going somewhere and no one sat watching. This disturbed her. She felt herself to be far, far away from everything she had ever known." Most importantly, she can find "no pattern" (*MM* 79) in American life, and the idea of pattern is essential to her sense of identity and purpose.

Both her identity and the purpose of her travels are closely related in Malika's imagination to her conception of home, which remains the Moroccan village she has left behind. When on the first day of her journey Tim suggests taking her home, she refuses to go back, but her idea of where her home is matches his at that moment. On the other hand, Tex's declaration that they are "going home" (*MM* 76), meaning to the United States, precipitates "a sinking sensation" (*MM* 76) in Malika because she knows that Tex's home is not her own. She even tells him, "But it's your house, not mine!" (*MM* 77). On the airplane bound for Los Angeles, her awareness of being away from home becomes suddenly intense: "She shut her eyes and sat quietly, feeling she had gone much too far away—so far that now she was nowhere. Outside the world, she whispered to herself in Arabic, and shivered" (*MM* 76). Arriving in Los Angeles, Malika is convinced that she has "left behind everything that was comprehensible, and was now in a totally different place whose laws she could not know" (*MM* 77). Again after Tex's death, she feels that she has "gone too far for the possibility of return" (*MM* 84). All of these reflections suggest that Malika's colonizing mission is no more successful than those of other Bowles characters like the Moresbys. She carries with her a conception of home, her personal "inside," but she is unable to extend it; indeed, she may have gone too far into the snowstorm to find her way back to the window.

When Malika does attempt to recover her sense of home, the purpose behind her movements, long hidden, at last becomes apparent:

> It was true that she was going back to help her mother; she was going because it was included in the pattern. Since the day she had run away, the vision of the triumphant return had been with her, when she would be living proof that her mother had been mistaken, that she was not like the other girls of the town. (*MM* 93)

The story's whole plot has sprung from that one stinging slap on the face, the point at which Malika's home ceased to be familiar to her. Like so many other people in Bowles she has set out to find that Bachelardian center of repose and comfort which, if it exists at all, can be found only in imagination. All along the way she keeps the image in her mind, and it sustains her. But she is finally unable either to project it onto the alien world she penetrates or to rediscover it when she returns to Morocco. The pattern is broken, unfamiliar. Instead of "the little house above the gully" (*MM* 91) she finds a "meaningless terrain" of rubble. Her outsidedness is complete.

The idea of the foreign in Bowles obviously extends beyond the political. But reaching out into alien territory is so often couched in cultural terms that it would be a mistake to treat the cultural dimension as exclusively metaphorical. Having spent nearly all his adult life traveling in strange lands, Bowles is well positioned for his role as one of this century's most astute observers of interaction between people of vastly different backgrounds, and particularly between westerners and residents of third world countries. "Here to Learn" is an excellent case in point. Malika's often comical attempts to cross the threshold of seemingly impenetrable cultural interiors are an essential part of the story's meaning. Malika looks at Europeans and sees women with "the pelts of animals over their shoulders" (*MM* 62) and people with "long boards on their feet" (*MM* 64) at a ski resort, but despite her initial lack of understanding, she does not give up her mission of domestication. She wears western clothes, takes skiing lessons, and learns to speak English. All of these efforts are ultimately in vain, since she never feels truly at home in the west, and indeed, by the end of the story, her deracination is complete.

"You Have Left Your Lotus Pods on the Bus" may be Bowles' lightest treatment of cultural barriers. The plot is simple. Two Americans working in Thailand go on an outing with a Buddhist monk and two novices. In contrast to many Bowles stories, this one does not move toward disaster or a condition of utter exposure and isolation. The expedition is a success, and the travelers return safely to Bangkok. But during the course of the day the Americans, through a series of comical exchanges with the Thais, show how completely they are strangers in a strange land. The monk Yamyong, for instance, asks about the significance inherent in the various ways of wearing a necktie. He is told to his surprise that there is none. Later, on the bus to Ayudhaya, Thailand's ancient capital, the narrator makes a perfectly serious remark about the temples and buffalo they see along the way, and Yamyong is inexplicably amused. Conversely, a menu with items like "Shrimps Balls and Green Marrow" (CS 397) provokes the Americans to laughter while the Thais sit in stony silence. The monk and novices also seem to disapprove of the Americans' eating lunch, although they say nothing. Finally, on the way back, the narrator and his compatriot are astonished by a man screaming loudly from the back of the bus. They later are told that he is neither crazy nor drunk, as they had thought, but merely "busy." He was doing his job—to watch the road and shout instructions at the driver. Why he could not sit up front *with* the driver is not explained to the satisfaction of the Americans, or indeed, to that of the reader, who is drawn by the first-person narrator into a nearly continuous web of misunderstanding.

The difficulties of imaginatively annexing a different cultural realm have continued to disturb and preoccupy Bowles. In a short interview with Harvey Breit over thirty years ago, he expounded on the particular problems involved in attempting to understand Moslems:

> I don't think we're likely to get to know the Moslems very well, and I suspect that if we should we'd find them less sympathetic than we do at present. And I believe the same applies to their getting to know us. At the moment they admire us for our technique; I don't think they could find more than that compatible. Their culture is essentially barbarous, their mentality that of a purely predatory people.[13]

As time passed, Bowles' understanding of Moroccan life seems to have expanded, and his view of Moslems has certainly softened. A new edition of *Their Heads Are Green and Their Hands Are Blue* omits one essay, "Mustapha and His Friends," that expresses similar sentiments. But it would be a mistake to conclude that Bowles no longer recognizes the barriers implicit in the passage quoted above. In a much more recent interview he was asked about the possibility of a "Western-style relationship" with a Moroccan and replied, "No, no. That's an absurd concept. Like expecting a boulder to spread its wings and fly away." [14] After four decades of virtually continuous residence in Morocco, Bowles still acknowledges that he is an outsider; but he nonetheless writes with the authority of one who has studied the inside with some care.

Bowles calls his most recent book, *Points in Time,* "a lyrical history." [15] It is in fact a series of vignettes drawn from two millennia of Moroccan history and tradition. His selection of these episodes for retelling testifies forcefully that his efforts to make Moroccan society more comprehensible to westerners have not abated. He himself (unlike some of his characters) has not been defeated by the attempt to make the foreign less strange. Furthermore, although the stories in *Points in Time* are retellings, they read almost as if they were Bowles originals, in that they involve journeys into unknown regions and the problems that such journeys bring about. It would seem that even when working with material that is not purely fictional, Bowles' imagination discovers patterns that correspond to his own experience. The protagonist of one of these tales, a sixteenth-century Franciscan monk, is almost a prototype for the Bowles explorer—almost, in fact, an avatar of Bowles himself. Through the aid of a highly educated Moroccan acquaintance, Fra Andrea arranges to travel to Fez, where he plans to set up a small mission and get to know the country by "having religious discussions" [16] with Moslem intellectuals. But true to form, everything goes wrong. By the time Fra Andrea and his two companions arrive in Fez, a new sultan has come to power, and the atmosphere is not nearly so friendly as they anticipated. Fra Andrea is reduced to making intellectual contacts in the Mellah (the Jewish quarter) where he feels more comfortable, but even there he is distrusted. The religious discussions he has envisioned do take place. On a number of occasions he argues theology with several Moroccan rabbis. His intellect is so acute, however, and his command of logic so great, that the superstitious Moroccans think him to be in league with Satan. They complain to the Moslem authorities, who, happy to be rid of him, torture the monk, and impale him on a lance.

Another segment of *Points in Time,* one set several centuries later, takes up the question of outsidedness even more directly. In this tale a Jewish girl in Fez, in defiance of her parents' wishes, leaves the Mellah to marry a young Moslem. Her journey out, no less than that of Fra Andrea, leads to disaster. In some ways Sol Hachuel's situation is similar to Malika's in "Here to Learn." Like Malika, Sol is a victim of her beauty, which quickly becomes "legendary throughout the city" (*PT* 51). And also like Malika, Sol finds that her beauty draws her out, away from the security of her family home. Mohammed Zrhouni, who is already indisposed to taking a Moslem bride "since that would involve the word of his female relations as to the girl's desirability" (*PT* 51), is attracted to Sol. The "inevitable" occurs one day when Sol goes "out of the house" (*PT* 52) and does not return. She marries Mohammed and is converted to Islam. But Mohammed's family believe, "like most Moslems, that no Jew's conversion to Islam could be considered authentic" (*PT* 51). This apparently offhand statement is vital to the story's development. Can anyone really belong somewhere else? Can the alien be made familiar? Sol finds that it cannot, and her feeling of not belonging is intensified by her being forbidden to go outside the house. In short, she has gone too far into foreign territory; she cannot return. Her husband tells her that a woman "goes out" only three times; when she leaves her mother's womb, when she leaves her father's house, and when she leaves this world. But Sol escapes and returns briefly to her family. Her first journey, to Mohammed's house, leads her into a world her imagination cannot domesticate; her second leads to her beheading by a Moslem military guard.

These are among Bowles' nightmare stories; not all of his tales of cultural interaction are so grisly. In "The Time of Friendship" the visitor to North Africa is a Swiss schoolteacher who spends her winters in the Sahara.[17] Fräulein Windling, rather like the Moresbys in *The Sheltering Sky*, thinks: "What we have lost, they still possess" (*CS* 388). More than a few journeys out in Bowles are motivated by a discontent with western culture and a belief, always mistaken, that a new home can be found among the "primitive." Cultural and psychological implications coalesce at this point. Fundamentally, the flight is toward a home to replace the one that has failed—a desperate reaching outside for a new interior. Fräulein Windling's attempt is a valiant one, and it comes closer to success than most such efforts in Bowles' fiction. She fashions a kind of family composed of herself and the native boy Slimane. She buys him gifts, invites him to her house, takes him on excursions. She seems to be breaking through the barriers. But one year at Christmas she makes a crèche. Her purpose is to make Slimane understand her religion—to let him into a corner of her western house that still feels comfortable to her. Their conversations about religion have always been marked by misunderstanding, and she means to correct this failure. When she leaves Slimane in the room with the crèche while she fetches her flash attachment, the boy, who has had no dinner that day, demolishes the crèche and eats the fruits, nuts, and candies inside. The Fräulein reflects that "she had come to think of him as being very nearly like herself" and that "he had been undergoing a process of improvement as a result of knowing her" (*CS* 354). If by "improvement" she means westernization, she may be right in a sense, despite Slimane's destruction of the crèche. As the story closes, Fräulein Windling has been ordered to leave Algeria and Slimane has left his peaceful, "primitive" village to join the rebels fighting in the north. The ending of the story is paradoxical. On the one hand, Slimane's taking up arms against the French can be seen as a more deliberate and purposeful assault on western culture than his attack on the crèche, while, on the other hand, by joining the fighting he leaves behind a traditional way of life that he will probably never see again, even if he survives. As in *The Spider's House,* modernization under colonial rule seems destined to be replaced by modernization after independence.

One of Bowles' earliest published stories, "Tea on the Mountain," displays another kind of cultural interaction. Here, too, a woman (this time an American) finds herself befriending a young North African, but the setting is Tangier in the thirties, and the process of westernization is far more advanced than it is in Fräulein Windling's remote Saharan village. "Tea on the Mountain" contains an extraordinary number of allusions to various kinds of communication—novel writing, the wailing of muezzins, letters, cables, a flashing lighthouse, body language—and communication is what the story is centrally about. When the American woman first meets Mjid and his fat, slow-witted friend Ghazi, she notices that they have an understanding of one another that transcends the occasional misstatement or inappropriate remark. Such understanding, however, is made possible by an intricate web of social conventions that the woman can only observe, not share.

This becomes evident on the next day. The three have agreed to go on a picnic together. The young Moroccans are comparatively affluent, and, like many of their class, they are eager to adopt western customs. They insist, for example, that the woman bring ham and wine on the picnic, even though both are expressly forbidden to Moslems by the Koran. Ghazi drinks too much wine and falls asleep, leaving the woman and Mjid to wander around the farm owned by Mjid's family. Bowles makes it clear throughout the story that the social web that binds the young Moroccans together is fragile, and that it is threatened by the intrusive effect of western values. Another web is being woven between Mjid and the American, but this one is even more delicate because it is one-sided. Mjid goes more than halfway as he expresses his eagerness to visit her in America and "bring back cinema stars and presents from New York" (CS 24). She, in turn, tells herself that she is with Mjid because she does not and cannot know him. This gives her a feeling of freedom rather akin to the condition to which Nelson Dyar aspires in *Let It Come Down*. Mjid is prepared to reach out from his safe, traditional world, whatever the dangers, and he, not the American visitor, is the story's true adventurer. But there is a sadness and poignancy about Mjid's situation. The cultural framework he wishes to adopt, epitomized by the American woman, has no real place for him, and he will never feel comfortable in it; yet his own traditional society is slipping away.

"Tea on the Mountain" ends with a forceful restatement of the distance between Mjid and the American. She looks at his face and murmurs "a word without knowing what it was." She repeats the word: "incredible" (CS 22). Not long afterward she tells Mjid that she must leave for Paris immediately. He gives her a card on which he writes the address of his room in the Casbah. This little room, which he keeps a secret even from his family, is the key to his sense of identity. It is his place, his truest home. Under the address he writes the word "incredible" and underlines it twice. After he leaves she tosses "the white card" (CS 25) on the edge of the bed, where it hovers, about to fall on the floor. All that is most important to Mjid, all that he wished to share with the American woman, is reduced in a single deft phrase to a white piece of paper. With such swiftness and ease human meaning is supplanted by the blankness that lies all around.

Although published some fifteen years earlier, "Tea on the Mountain" adumbrates *The Spider's House* more exactly than any of Bowles' other stories. The Moroccan caught between two cultures and the detached westerner who eventually abandons him are the essential components of both the story and the novel. But *The Spider's House* is a far more richly suggestive work, with its fuller treatment of modern Moroccan life and its larger cast of characters. The western visitors in the novel are a diverse lot with differing motives for being in North Africa. Stenham's British friends, Moss and Kenzie, appear to disagree in their attitudes toward the Moroccans, although their disagreement is largely superficial. Moss, a wealthy painter, is openly pro-French. Rather like a more subdued and polite version of the vitriolic Ellis in Orwell's *Burmese Days,* he thinks that a "clout on the head works wonders" (*SH* 154). Moss sees Moroccan culture, in Stenham's words, as "something accidentally left over from bygone centuries" (*SH* 155) that will inevitably perish if the Europeans impose sufficient discipline. Kenzie on the other hand fancies himself on the Moroccan side (even though he does not hesitate to roar ostentatiously around Fez in an MG). When the summer's turmoil becomes truly dangerous, the two men's stances shift somewhat. Kenzie is the first to bolt Fez for the safety of Tangier and the International Zone, while Moss, having seen Moroccans tortured, exclaims that "the French have lost their minds" (*SH* 231).

Stenham alone has an appreciation of Moroccan culture, but even his attitudes are ambiguous. He refuses to drink alcohol with Moroccan cuisine (presumably because it would be a culinary defilement of some sort), and he deplores the modernizing tendencies of the Istiqlal (Independence) party, but when a Moroccan boy scratches his name, Mohammed, on Kenzie's MG, it is Stenham, not Moss, who berates the child, citing the car's cost and the cost of repairs. Despite his romanticizing of traditional Moroccan culture, which becomes evident in his arguments with Lee, Stenham seems to have a strange attachment to symbols of western materialism. Even his romantic regard for Moroccan tradition does not originate in any sense of identification with it. He dines regularly at Si Jaffar's house, and he temporarily takes up with Amar, but he never ceases to think of himself as an outsider, an observer, "of nothing, free" (*SH* 166). His flight to the modern, French-built city of Casablanca at the novel's end is a return to the world from which he came. Like Fielding in *A Passage to India*, Stenham fails to bridge a cultural gap. But unlike him, Stenham lives in a less innocent time when modest attempts at understanding are not enough. Recognition of this harsh fact is a major source of the cynicism and detachment that keep him from success but, paradoxically, also protect him. Lee's domesticating mission differs strategically from Stenham's, and its failure is less pronounced. If Stenham has tried to "know" the traditional Morocco, to feel at home there, Lee has insisted, like Moss, that the old Morocco is doomed. In arguing that the country must be modernized, she represents the tendency to extend the boundaries of the domestic—to make the foreign less strange by transforming it into the familiar. Hers is the impulse that leads June to redecorate Van's apartment in "How Many Midnights." It is the classic imperialist position. As the book draws to a close, with Morocco poised for further social change, it appears that this form of domestication may, in the long run, achieve a measure of success.

The price of that success, Stenham knows, is the destruction of a culture that has served as an effective social shelter for centuries. It is no accident, therefore, that the novel's real focus is on Amar, through whose experiences the reader sees the destruction most vividly. Amar is an outsider in several ways. Most obviously, the western culture that is enveloping his country is making his own "house" increasingly strange to him. The contrast between his traditional mode of perception and the European ways he observes adds both poignancy and humor to the novel, in much the same manner that the same combination does in "Here to Learn." When Amar first catches sight of Lee Burroughs he thinks she is "a prostitute of the lowest order" (*SH* 137) because she wears a sleeveless dress or a worker in the fields because she has a suntan. He disapproves of the changes he witnesses, yet he seems fated to be swept up in them. The fictional Amar's situation parallels that

of the real Abdeslam, except that Abdeslam found Islamic culture in Istanbul disintegrating much more rapidly than in Morocco. Bowles, in *Their Heads Are Green and Their Hands Are
Blue,* reflects on that revelation with great sympathy:

> Abdeslam is not a happy person. He sees his world, which he knows
> is a good world, being assailed from all sides, slowly crumbling be-
> fore his eyes. . . . Something will have to be found to replace the
> basic wisdom which has been destroyed, but the discovery will not
> be soon; neither Abdeslam nor I will ever know of it. (p. 82)

In all probability Amar will never know it either. For the time
being he is fated to walk through unfamiliar territory. His desire
for European shoes is only one small sign that he will, along with
the rest of Morocco, step out of the shelter of a traditional culture and into the wilderness of a modern one.

But even within that traditional culture Amar is an outsider.
He bitterly resents his inferior status as a second son. Even
though he knows he is more worthy, his elder brother Mustapha
is given preferential treatment by his father. This is one custom
that Amar examines critically and rather rationally. Another is
the wild folk dancing at a Moslem festival Amar attends with
Stenham and Lee. "It makes you sick to your stomach to look at
it," he says later, "all those people jumping up and down like
monkeys" (*SH* 369). What is most significant about the remark
is that he makes it to Moulay Ali, a leader of the Istiqlal, which
advocates both independence and modernization. When he is
locked out of the medina (and consequently, out of his father's
house), Amar's drift toward the new order accelerates. His attachment to Stenham is nonetheless ironic, since Stenham is not
only an American but also a man who rather prides himself on
his aloofness from his fellow human beings.

Many years ago Paul Bowles acquired a small island in what is
now Sri Lanka. He later explained the purchase as an unsuc-
cessful attempt at personal colonization: "I've never thought
anything belonged to me. At one time, I bought an island off
Ceylon and I thought that when I had my two feet planted on it
I'd be able to say: 'This island is mine.' I couldn't. It was meaningless." [18] The underlying idea in the anecdote is that homelessness is an ineradicable fact of human life. It is difficult not to

draw the same conclusion from Amar's outsidedness at the end of *The Spider's House*. Amar desperately wants to stay with Stenham, but the Americans, having let him ride with them a short way, rudely put him out of their car. He is left to watch the automobile move swiftly away. "Allah's most terrible punishment," his father has told him once, is to be "in the street without friends, without clothes, without a mat to lie on, without a piece of bread, alive but not really alive, dead but not even dead" (*SH* 378). This, at least in a figurative sense, is Amar's condition. When Stenham tells him it is a long way to walk back, he replies, "Back to where?" (*SH* 404). Like Malika in "Here to Learn," he finds that there "is no reason to do anything" (*SH* 374) without the protective forms that give meaning and shape to life. When Amar makes his first appearance in the novel, he considers running away from the security of home but decides against it. Now that there is nowhere to go, the continuation of his journey out is inevitable. He has become, by necessity, another one of Paul Bowles' explorers.

4. The Shapes of Bowles' Fiction

FOR A WRITER who suspects, like the Owl in *The Thousand and One Nights,* that the world is a vast emptiness built upon emptiness, a problem of plot construction arises: how to represent metaphysical vacancy in fictional form. How is a world that seems irrefutably open to be rendered artistically—in effect, to be sufficiently enclosed for intelligibility—without falsifying the artist's own sense of reality? Both Marianna Torgovnick and John Kucich, in separate discussions of Frank Kermode, comment on this dilemma. Torgovnick asserts that "all human fictions" are torn "between the desire to mime contingency and disorder and the opposing need to create coherence and system."[1] The novelist, Kucich agrees (again paraphrasing Kermode), seeks to impose order on the chaos of experience but also seeks "to bring such order closer and closer to experiential chaos."[2] The paradox particularly besets postmodernist writers, many of whom confront vacancy of meaning and a sense of exteriority by means of plot structures that resist usual patterns of order.

Bowles' fictions have, in general, been perceived as formally traditional. Yet there is within them a tension between openness and closure—a tension that reflects the effort to tell a story both lifelike (to be truthful) and unlifelike (to be comprehensible). Bowles' work is delicately poised between the unacceptable chaos of experience and the unbelievable order of artifice. It must partake of each, because in novels, as Philip Stevick says, "accommodation must be made between 'the continuity of things' . . . and the 'geometry' of art."[3] Stevick discusses narrative art (using Wilhelm Worringer's helpful terminology) as tending chiefly toward the pole of "empathy" without ever abandoning the pole of pure abstraction that gives it shape and meaning. What we find in Bowles' stories and novels are certain features that contribute to centripetal plot movement, toward closure, resolution, shape, and meaning, and certain others that seem to accelerate centrifugal movement toward openness, irresolution, and vacancy. These elements are often inextricably entwined. In short, his plots contain structural traces of his primary artistic "figure": the opposition between inside and out. An important point to recall while examining these structural matters is that the story itself, however "open," is finally an attempt at some kind of closure, however tentative. To tell any story is to domesticate experience through articulation, to bring it into the familiar interiors of human comprehension. But storytelling as the most pervasive and accessible human shelter is a subject that must be given a chapter of its own.

I. CENTRIPETAL MOVEMENT: ENCLOSURE

Centripetal movement in narrative includes all ways of shaping, whether consciously understood or merely intuited by the reader, that heighten the sense of authorial presence, deliberate construction, and containment. In Bowles' fiction this effect is achieved largely through the traditional methods of narrative division, manipulation of point of view, the arrangement of narrative sequence, and the modulation of narrative pace. Because *The Spider's House* employs all of these techniques extensively, I will concentrate my discussion of centripetal structures there. Clearly demarcated narrative divisions or subsections are the most immediately apparent structuring principle in *The Spider's House,* and they characterize all of Bowles' other novels as well. Here, these divisions are so manifestly discrete that the spaces between them seem almost geographical boundaries. They are even somewhat quaintly called "books." Each section, with the exception of the first, begins with its own epigraph and title, suggesting an individual character that is part of, yet distinct from, the narrative as a whole. If Stevick is correct in maintaining that "chapter division and chapter construction are expressive techniques that demonstrate, at every point, the conscious shaping of form" (*CF* 103), then surely larger, more pronounced divisions display that shaping even more patently.

The first division's simple designation, "Prologue," indicates that its action stands in a different relation to the rest of the narrative than any of the four long subsections. The plot of the prologue is very simple. John Stenham departs from Si Jaffar's house after dinner one summer night, walks through the medina, and finds at his hotel a message to the effect that Moss must see him at once. Although action in these ten pages is scant, much is suggested that reverberates later in the novel. Si Jaffar's insistence on sending a guide with Stenham (even though he knows the way) and the guide's unusually circuitous route hint of dangers on which much of the novel's larger plot hinges. The architecture of the medina, so nearly enclosed yet so open to the sky, prepares the reader for the novel's major theme of the inadequacy of humanly fashioned shelters. And Stenham's own outsidedness, his movement from a comparatively safe house (where, ironically, he does not really belong) to his hotel room (where ominous news awaits) prefigures all the journeys out in *The Spider's House:* Stenham's, Lee's, and particularly Amar's.

None of this is apparent at first because the prologue abruptly ends as Stenham enters Moss's room, and Book One, "The Master of Wisdom," begins. Each of the novel's books has a focal point indicated by the author's choice of title and epigraph. "The Master of Wisdom" introduces Amar, the child who is wise enough to choose Allah as his patron. His fixed moral code drawn from centuries-old religious and cultural traditions provides him with a sense of safety, of enclosure, that the novel's European and American characters lack. He is also wise enough to be dimly aware "that the world is a vast emptiness built upon emptiness" (*SH* 12), as the section's epigraph states. At one point he reflects that this world "was approaching its end, and beyond was unfathomable darkness" (*SH* 47). Taken by itself, this part of the novel could be read as a self-sufficient story about the difficulty of maintaining one's faith while surrounded by evidence that faith is everywhere eroding.

The decline of faith is central also to the next section (as indeed it is, in a more general sense, to the entire novel). In "Sins Are Finished" Amar's story is continued from the spring to the summer of 1954 and the crisis of August, when there was no legitimate sultan to sacrifice a sheep at the Aïd el Kebir. The title refers to the words of Amar's employer, the potter Said, who declares that without the true sultan nothing matters any more: "Sins are finished!" (*SH* 114) as well as to the subsequent words of Amar's father: "There is sin everywhere now" (*SH* 121). Amar realizes that these two apparently contradictory statements mean the same thing. The epigraph directly addresses the question of the meaning of words:

> You tell me you are going to Fez.
> Now, if you say you are going to Fez,
>   That means you are not going.
> But I happen to know that you are going to Fez.
> Why have you lied to me, you who are my friend? (*SH* 55)

The distinction between truth and fiction becomes particularly important in this section, as Amar struggles to maintain his allegiance to a conception of the real and the true: the metaphysical meaning that lies beyond the fallacies and contradictions inherent in human articulation.

"Sins Are Finished" concludes with Amar's observation of two Americans who have taken refuge from a riot in the café where he is having tea. The couple are identified in the next book as John Stenham and Lee Burroughs. From here on, Stenham's story is joined with Amar's. "The Hour of the Swallows" fills in Stenham's activities during the past several weeks (including the events described in the prologue) and climaxes with his meeting with Amar in the café. The swallows of the title are both Stenham and Amar, as is evident from the epigraph:

> To my way of thinking, there is nothing more delightful than to be a stranger. And so I mingle with human beings, because they are not of my kind, and precisely in order to be a stranger among them.
> —Song of the Swallow
> The Thousand and One Nights (*SH* 141)

The reference is more immediately applicable to Stenham, who seeks out the foreign partly "in order to be a stranger." Amar finds himself a stranger against his will and derives little delight from it, as he falls under the protection of the Americans after being locked out of the medina. His dependence on Stenham, as well as their continuing strangeness to one another, adumbrates much that will happen to his country in the near future. Certainly this section's focus is the ineradicability of that strangeness.

The title of the concluding book, "The Ascending Stairways," returns to the Koran—source of the novel's title and epigraph. Here the relevant passage again warns those "who choose other patrons than Allah": "A questioner questioned concerning the doom about to fall upon the disbelievers, which none can repel, from Allah, Lord of the Ascending Stairways" (*SH* 265). Standing at the head of the novel, a similar warning seems directed exclusively and unambiguously at the secularizers within Moroccan society. But by Book Four secularization itself is so ascendant that the admonition seems laden with irony. As Amar and Stenham part, reunite, and part again, the dominant impression is not that of a triumphant Islamic society putting unbelievers to flight, but of that society itself in a state of rapid deterioration. In this book as in each of the others, the title and epigraph focus the reader's attention in a way that emphasizes the conscious selection and arrangement of materials and increases a comfortable sense of experience as construct.

I have stressed the "shapefulness" of each of the major subsections and its importance in the gathering up of the novel's meanings, images, and events into an intelligible whole. But it should also be noted that none of the novel's books can stand alone. Each is open-ended and dependent upon another block of narrative for completion. The prologue ends abruptly in the middle of a conversation that is not resumed until the middle of Book Two—some two hundred pages later. Book One is the most nearly self-contained section, but it, too, has an open ending. Amar finds his broher Mustapha smoking kif on the terrace one night and asks him if he needs it to sleep. Mustapha angrily tells him to go to bed, and Amar has "one more thing to think about" (*SH* 54) as he falls asleep. Mustapha's newly acquired kif habit is "one more" sign that Amar's world is crumbling apart. A more ominous sign, and one that contributes far more to Amar's sleeplessness, is the increase in Istiqlal bombings. Amar finds it difficult to understand how Moslems can kill other Moslems, even in the cause of independence. The mounting political tension, recorded both in conversation and in Amar's thoughts, makes a quick dramatic resolution increasingly implausible, and certainly nothing is resolved by Amar's dropping off to sleep one unremarkable night.

The next book moves swiftly into a summer of escalating violence and terror and to the novel's central day, when Amar encounters two Americans, a man and a woman, in a café outside the walls of the medina. A riot is gathering momentum in the streets, and all three are in the café waiting for the clamor to abate. Amar observes the American couple at length before walking into another room. As he returns to the original room, the section ends. Bringing "Sins Are Finished" to such an inconclusive conclusion is a masterful stroke. Everything and nothing has happened. In a sense, the "end" of this book is the meeting of Amar and Stenham, but that end is withheld until Book Three. In the same manner, the "end" of "The Master of Wisdom," the event toward which the political tension builds, is the riot that takes place only in Book Two. The pattern is repeated once more in "The Hour of the Swallows," which doubles back to a point earlier in the summer and tracks Stenham's and Lee's movements through the scene in the café. The Americans agree to take Amar back to the hotel with them (since he is shut out of the medina and cannot go home), but the results of this decision, and the implications of Amar and Stenham's meeting, are not revealed until the novel's final section. The last book takes up the consequences of the meeting, but it offers no real resolution, ending as it does with Amar simply abandoned, left behind in the empty road. But unlike the preface and first three books, "The Ascending Stairways" looks forward to no postponed resolution. All the other major subdivisions have open endings that are closed at a later stage in the text. The final book has an open ending that is not closed. And the utter blankness at the novel's end seems all the more stark precisely because those earlier blanknesses are eventually filled in. The partitioning of the novel's material into these subsections, these rooms, and the effort to close off (however belatedly) each section suggest a house that has been carefully and methodically shut up for the winter, with only the back door—or perhaps a back window— left open.

The other major ways in which Bowles organizes and gathers narrative—the arrangement of sequence, the modulation of pace, and the alternation of point of view—are closely connected to one another in *The Spider's House*. The novel opens with a prologue involving Stenham, and the point of view in this section is entirely Stenham's. For more than a hundred pages after the prologue, however, Stenham's story is suspended while the story of Amar (told from Amar's viewpoint) is developed. The Amar narrative in its turn is dropped, at the conclusion of Book Two, and the reader, expecting some kind of structural enclosure or at least a connection between Amar and Stenham, might reasonably wonder if the plots will ever merge. The blocks of narrative are finally linked, and the two stories join, but not before Bowles has definitively established the solidity of Amar's and Stenham's separate worlds. After the meeting in the café, point of view continues to alternate, but in shorter segments. Some of the later events of the novel are also seen through Lee's eyes, but by the end the center of consciousness is again Amar.

Shifts in point of view are complicated by a great deal of what Gérard Genette calls anachrony: "forms of discordance between the two temporal orders of story and narrative." By "story" Genette refers to the sequence in which events purportedly happen, and by "narrative," to the sequence in which they are related. Two of the most frequently occurring forms of anachrony are prolepsis, "any narrative maneuver that consists of narrating or evoking in advance an event that will take place later," and analepsis, "any evocation after the fact of an event that took place earlier than the point in the story where we are at any given moment."[4] Analepsis first occurs (along with a shift in point of view) after the prologue ends, when the narrative moves back to a point in the story that is much earlier—the spring day on which Amar is introduced. Narrative sequence and story sequence are largely identical during Books One and Two, which take Amar through the summer to the fateful day in August when he meets Stenham. But at the beginning of Book Three there is another major analeptic shift back to a day some weeks before the meeting, and the point of view is once more Stenham's. Toward the end of Book Three the narrative catches up with the story, and from here on a high degree of synchrony is maintained through several changes in point of view until the end of the novel. These discordances serve different functions. The first analepsis fills in Amar's background and, in so doing, brings to life the social and political milieu in which Stenham finds himself. The second, on the other hand, reveals all that is necessary about the background and attitudes of the man on whom Amar will come to depend—and, by implication, the cultural values that Morocco seems ultimately destined to adopt. But these are largely thematic functions. The careful delineation of units of time, the stopping and starting, backing and filling, also suggest, if only subliminally, that experience, however ragged, can be shaped.

Shlomith Rimmon-Kenan has noted that both prolepsis and analepsis can result in "hermeneutic gaps" in the text that may or may not be filled in. An analepsis, she explains, "often fills-in an anterior gap, but it may also create a new gap by giving a different slant to already-narrated events, thus making it difficult to reconcile fresh impressions with 'old' ones" (*NF* 128–129). This type of gap is usually temporary, as we can see in *The Spider's House*. When Stenham's walk back from Si Jaffar's to his hotel suddenly yields, at the beginning of Book One, to a day in Amar's life several months earlier, there is an empty space where the reader expects information. The filling in of that particular gap does not even begin to occur until near the end of Book Two, when it becomes evident that the American man Amar observes in the café is Stenham. A similar gap falls between Books Two and Three, when the narrative again returns to an earlier point in time, in this instance centering on Stenham. Both gaps are eventually filled in, but they stand as temporary pauses before a starting over, reasserting both the authority of a storyteller who is a master of space and time and the shapefulness of the story he fashions. Yet they are indeed holes in the fabric of narrative and, as such, they also stand as reminders of the nothing that narrative covers—the vast emptiness of the world.

Another temporal aspect of Bowles' fiction that contributes to a sense of shape has to do with the pace of narrative. Bowles himself has commented on the importance of this element in his work, and he sees it as a direct result of his experience as a composer. Musical form, he explained, "*is* form, as far as I'm concerned. Yes, form as I see it has to do with the sense of speed, that is, the relationship between what's going on in the book and the duration of time it takes to tell it. And to read it."⁵ As Genette points out, there is no accurate way of measuring text duration, since telling time (which must be conceived as reading time) varies from reader to reader. One can, however, posit a "*conventional* equality between narrative time and story time" and consider departures from it: "The isochronous narrative, our hypothetical reference zero, would thus be here a narrative with unchanging speed, without accelerations or slowdowns, where the relationship duration-of-story/length-of-narrative would remain always steady" (*ND* 86–88). *The Spider's House* perhaps comes closest to this state in the prologue. One can well imagine that Stenham's walk through the medina takes approximately as long in the story as the telling of it, allowing for Stenham's reflections along the way. But with Book One the pace is radically accelerated, as months of Amar's life pass in just forty pages. Even within this segment of narrative, of course, the pace of many individual scenes is slowed—as if by a film projectionist or orchestra conductor—to the point at which narrative time greatly exceeds story time. Generally speaking, the weeks and months preceding Amar and Stenham's meeting are related much more rapidly than the events occur. Although many scenes are slowed down, the frequent use of ellipsis (in effect, "skipping" from one scene, one temporal frame, to another with a minimum of narration) makes the overall pace of these sections quite rapid. But the central period of the novel's action—the day before the meeting, the day of the meeting, and the three days that follow—is narrated much more slowly. Those five days of story time take up nearly three hundred pages of text. These carefully contrived fluctuations in the rhythm of the novel—so different from the way in which time is experienced in life—make the reader all the more sensible of the shaping, building, arranging, enclosing processes that Bowles simply calls form.

Most of these centripetal structural features can be found in Bowles' three other novels as well. *Up Above the World,* for instance, is a bewildering web of shifts in sequence and point of view. Although Bowles has downplayed the seriousness of this highly entertaining study of a psychopathic killer, preliminary

notes in the Humanities Research Center reveal that it was meticulously constructed, and that point of view was of central importance from the book's inception. Bowles' concept was of a novel

> in which the story-line is apparently about two or more other people.
> The narrator participates in the story-line and records episodes.
> Thus constantly adjusting time point, to allow for alternate use of
> present and past. That the dénouement of each episode is a result of
> careful manipulation on the part of narrator is made clear each time,
> but casually, thrown away.[6]

Everything in this description corresponds to the completed text
of *Up Above the World* except the reference to the narrator as a
participant. Bowles seldom uses a first-person, participatory narrator in his fiction and has never done so in a novel. Evidently he
decided against such a strategy in this case too. What he did do
was to make Grove Soto a malevolent center of consciousness.
The "other people" are the ostensible protagonists, Taylor and
Day Slade, who stumble into Soto's snares. While the "time
point" is constantly adjusted by the narrator, it is usually Soto
himself who manipulates the novel's various denouements—his
mother's murder, the Slade's visit to his house, Taylor's illness, the
prolongation of the visit, Taylor's death, Day's death. Those ma-
nipulations become increasingly frightening to the reader largely
because so much of the point of view is Soto's. Superficially the
plot of *Up Above the World* greatly resembles that of *The Sheltering Sky,* but the reader's experience is vastly different. A similar
effect is achieved in "The Circular Valley," where point of view is
centered on the Atlájala, a spirit who brings about the death of a
young man, and in "If I Should Open My Mouth," which has as
its narrator a psychopath who may also be a murderer. In each
case the reader is made privy to the perspective of the source of
danger.

Prolepsis and analepsis, the adjustment of the "time point"
that Bowles mentions in his notes, serve like other instances of
overt shaping to reinforce the impression of narrative as a construct. But they also tend to create, as in *The Spider's House,* significant gaps. If the arrangement of narrative around such gaps
suggests the architectural power of the storyteller, the gaps themselves suggest that which the architect cannot enclose. They are

what was there before words; they are what will be there after
words cease. It is fitting, then, that the gaps in *Up Above the
World* be so closely linked with death, the final silence and only
real security. Much of the novel's anachrony results from the deliberate withholding of direct information about the murders.
Bowles has spoken of "the value of the spaces between words."[7]
Gaps in narrative—not only in Bowles' work but in all fiction—
simultaneously heighten the reader's awareness of the presence of
story (the here, the known) and sharpen the reader's fear of the
terrible vacancies that story masks.

II. CENTRIFUGAL MOVEMENT: EXPOSURE

Those vacancies are suggested even more powerfully in Bowles
by the direction in which his plots move. All of Bowles' novels
and many of his stories have "open" plots that are not neatly
"tied up" at the end. Characters are left hanging; their conflicts
are left unresolved. There are, of course, different ways of defining open form. One of the best is that of Robert M. Adams, who
calls it "literary form (a structure of meanings, intents, and em-
phases, i.e., verbal gestures) which includes a major unresolved
conflict with the intent of displaying its unresolvedness."[8] My
concern is chiefly with the use (or non-use) of plot structure to
close off, contain, or otherwise bring to a sense of completion the
narrative as a whole. Perhaps the best illustration of the kind of
openness I mean is the end of Roman Polanski's film of *Macbeth*.
In the play major issues are resolved, at least provisionally, by the
death of Macbeth and the crowning of Malcolm at Scone. Polanski adds an extra scene in which Donalbain, on his way back
from Ireland, is himself tempted by the witches' prophecy. This
scene parallels Macbeth's initial rendezvous with the witches in
all essentials. The implication of Polanski's radically more open
ending is that nothing has been settled and that the cycle of violence and corruption will continue. The conclusion of *Up Above
the World* is similar to Polanski's. Grove Soto has killed the
Slades for fear that they know something about the murder of his
mother. But the drive for security, for total control over his life,
that motivates him throughout the novel cannot abate as long as
anyone is alive who knows the truth. And the final chapter ends

with his accomplice Thorny settling confidently into Soto's apartment. Whether Thorny will succeed in blackmailing Soto or will himself be murdered is left unanswered. In all probability Soto is another of Bowles' characters who has gone too far to return to a condition of presumed security. Every step takes him farther outward.

This journey out, as we have already seen, is the dominant plot structure in Bowles' fiction, and that plot lends itself especially well to the nonresolution of various conflicts. The movement of characters is from places and situations that seem safe and certain (or enclosed) to those that are clearly unsafe and uncertain (or exposed). The direction is always out into the open, either literally or metaphorically; and the journey home, back to the place of well-being and certitude, is usually thwarted in some way. Nothing makes this more apparent than the open window at the conclusion of "How Many Midnights." June's journey takes her gradually away from the security of her parents' home. Just as surely as Bowles' more obvious explorers, she attempts to colonize new territory (in her case, Van's life) even as she charts it. When the effort fails, she returns to her parents' apartment, but it will never be the same reassuring interior it once was. In a sense her return home anticipates Malika's in "Here to Learn." In the earlier story the physical dwelling remains intact, but June's experience leaves her as vulnerable and uncertain as Malika. What these kinds of endings often accomplish is a wrenching of the reader's entire perspective. As Philip Stevick explains it, "The open end is a formal shock, demanding of the reader an assimilation of the unexpected in a way that can challenge responses all the way from the reader's sober expectation of continuity to the reader's metaphysic. The open end . . . engages the reader's most basic and universal pattern-making impulses" (*CF* 73). Bowles' strategy in employing the open ending is nothing less than the simultaneous exposure and subversion of the human need for order.

The Sheltering Sky, Bowles' first extended narrative, illustrates as clearly as any of his works both the exposure and the subversion of that need. Because the return home—the implicit closure of every outward journey plot—becomes increasingly unlikely, the movement of *The Sheltering Sky* increasingly reveals itself as a centrifugal drift away from all forms of order. On the surface, signs of this drift proliferate. As the Moresbys move farther and farther from the Europeanized Mediterranean littoral, a long deterioration sets in that affects every aspect of the journey. Hotels become shabbier, less like home. Means of transportation become less comfortable, more dangerous. But beyond these obvious signs that the structures of civilization are falling away, a less visible dissolution is occurring. Neither Port nor Kit seems able to enter into the other's imaginative realm sufficiently to make their relationship work. Issues are raised by Port's visits to prostitutes and by Kit's brief affair with Tunner that are not allowed to be resolved. Port dies not knowing whether the marriage can be saved, and Kit wanders off at the end, hardly knowing even who she is. There is no returning home, either literally or metaphorically, and there is certainly no neat solution to the psychological or philosophical problems that are woven into the novel's texture.

But the plot of *The Sheltering Sky*, like those of Bowles' other novels, does at times approach closure. Two major episodes suggest safe return and the preservation of some semblance of order. Early in the book Port takes a walk through Oran, before the desert journey begins. The direction in which he walks leads him away from the European town near the sea and southward into the native quarter, toward the desert. This pattern prefigures the novel's larger one, as Port makes his way into the unknown and the uncontrollable. A stone hits him in the back, then a second on his leg. They are apparently not intended for him; two groups of children are engaged in battle with Port caught in their midst. The purposelessness of the incident only underscores its frightfulness. As Port walks on, the street becomes "constantly less urban," and the Milky Way appears in the night sky "like a giant rift across the heavens" (*SS* 25). A mysterious Arab, asking him the novel's key question, "*Qu'est-ce ti cherches?*" (*SS* 27), takes him deeper into the medina, where everything looks unfamiliar. Lawrence Stewart is correct in pointing out the similarity between these events and the opening of "A Distant Episode" (indeed, Bowles has done so himself), but he is wrong to assert that Port's walk has "no consequences for the novel" (*PB* 57). The importance of this incident lies in the very fact of Port's return. He places himself in danger, he becomes lost and is gone all night, but he does finally make his way safely back to the hotel. This segment of narrative, unlike the longer one that contains it, is closed.

Not long afterward Kit leaves her compartment on a south-bound train and walks up to the platform to a native car. Like Port, she leaves the security of a "European" area (the first-class coach on which she and Tunner are traveling) and moves into alien territory (a fourth-class coach occupied exclusively by Algerians). As she reboards the train, she is confronted by a thick swarm of Berbers and Arabs "milling about in the midst of a confusion of bundles and boxes, piled on the dirt platform under the faint light of a bare electric bulb" (SS 83). She enters the car, "crowded to bursting with men in dun-colored burnouses, squatting, sleeping, reclining, standing," and for the first time she feels "in a strange land" (SS 83–84). Scarcely understanding why she has come to this unfamiliar place, she finds herself "impelled forward in spite of all her efforts" (SS 84). The strangeness of her surroundings, and the feeling of purposelessness, of loss of control, parallel Port's earlier experience in Oran, and they are the essential characteristics of exposure in Bowles' fiction. Everything she observes strengthens the impression of unfamiliarity. A louse appears on her neck. The men stare at her with "the absorbed and vacant expression of the man who looks into his handkerchief after blowing his nose" (SS 84). She watches a man eating red locusts. She passes another man holding a severed sheep's head. And most tellingly, when she finally escapes to the platform again, she comes upon a man with "the most hideous human face she had ever seen" (SS 85). There is a triangular hole where his nose should be. She wonders why this diseased face should seem so much more horrible than a healthy one "whose expression reveals an interior corruption" (SS 86). The answer is contained in her very observation. She thinks of internal corruption because she sees external decay. The face, as in Pynchon's *V.*, is a cosmetic structure, flimsy and temporary at best, that barely contains the rot, the potential nothingness, beneath. It is at this point that Kit, with considerable determination, returns to the first-class coach and Tunner's embrace. As in the case of Port's walk, the return neatly closes off the episode, but not the larger narrative. The novel's greater estrangements continue to widen.

This variation on peripeteia, a temporary, provisional resolution, occurs frequently in Bowles' fiction and is always an important part of the work's centripetal force field. But premature closure also contributes to the narrative's ultimate centrifugal thrust in an indirect way. By closing off a smaller unit of narrative—one that suggests or parallels the pattern of the whole—Bowles increases the reader's expectation of further closure and thereby makes the inevitably open ending all the more striking. The technique is familiar to devotees of the horror film, in which the intensity of the final horror is often increased by making the protagonist appear safe and the dangerous situation appear defused (or closed) before the end. Bowles uses premature closure for more than just shock value. It is certainly true that Port's and Kit's safe returns from their brief excursions reinforce in the reader's mind an expectation of final return that is built into the conventions of travel literature. But the emptiness at the end where something is expected and even hoped for, the plot's final falling open into centrifugality despite all of its centripetal pressures, is also the deepest expression of Bowles' major theme.

Premature closure is most effective in Bowles' novels, where extended development, paralleling the development of the whole narrative, can be plotted out in discrete, closed episodes within the work. But Bowles sometimes uses the device with great skill in shorter pieces as well. "The Garden," a tale from the 1960's, is a good example. Spanning fewer than three pages of text, the story has only three characters who appear as individuals: a man, his wife, and the local imam. The man is so satisfied with the garden he has cultivated, his little domestication of the desert, that his wife thinks he has found a treasure and is keeping the secret from her. After consulting an old woman of the village she mixes a potion and begins to put it in her husband's food. Her aim is to induce him to tell her where the treasure is, but she succeeds only in making him extremely ill. The old woman advises her to flee before he dies. But the man recovers, and when he does he has lost much of his memory, including all recollection of his vanished wife. He has no friends because he recognizes no one, and he no longer goes to the mosque to pray. Although the townspeople and the imam grow suspicious of the man, he continues to work happily in his garden. With the wife, who is the original source of conflict, gone, the story seems on the verge of closure. Bowles' world, however, is the ragged, indeterminate world of the mid-twentieth century. Rewards and punishments are not this neatly apportioned, nor conflicts so easily resolved. That the seeming closure here is only temporary is strongly hinted by the villagers' and the imam's concerns. When the imam pays the man a second visit, he is astonished to find that the man has "never heard" (*CS* 365) of Allah. That night the people decide that the man can no longer live in the town. The next day a mob attacks him with stones, hoes, and sickles. After his death his small, cultivated enclosure, typical of so many in Bowles, is claimed by the great outside: "Little by little the trees died, and very soon the garden was gone. Only the desert was there" (*CS* 365). As in *The Sheltering Sky,* openness is displayed in different ways. Not only is the character's attempt at enclosure, his own little "tea in the Sahara," defeated, but the story's plot declines to snap shut at a point that would give the reader a sense of resolution.

This kind of tension between the centripetal and the centrifugal shapes the plot of *The Spider's House* as well. First, as we have observed, the novel's "books" are, to varying extents, closed-off units of narrative. Their closure is postponed until later sections, but it does occur. This is true of all but the last book, which bears the additional responsibility of concluding the whole novel. Neither the last part nor the whole is closed in the way that earlier sections are. Something similar happens when the novel is divided chronologically. While its central days, the five days surrounding and including Amar's meeting with Stenham, are clearly marked off and easy to discern, in terms of both their beginnings and their endings, the same cannot be said for the totality of the narrative. The beginning of Amar's story is indistinct—sometime in the spring of 1954—and its ending is left open. Stenham's story seems to begin, insofar as narrative chronology is concerned, a few weeks before he meets Amar, and his, too, is open-ended. By indistinct beginnings I mean that neither Amar's nor Stenham's first appearance in the chronological story can be pinpointed with accuracy. In short, great chronological specificity (contributing to closure) competes with considerable chronological vagueness (contributing to openness). And of course the openness inherent in Stenham's abandonment of Amar on the novel's last pages stands in such stark relief precisely because of the earlier temporary, insubstantial closure of their meeting.

Let It Come Down is Bowles' most self-consciously "de-signed" novel. "It was completely surface-built," he has ex-plained, "down to the details of the decor, choice of symbolic ma-terials on the walls, and so on. The whole thing was planned." [9] A look at his notes in the Humanities Research Center confirms these assertions. The alternation of point of view and the chro-nology of the initial chapters, for instance, are carefully lined up in a rather elaborate chart. But despite its meticulous construc-tion, the book also serves as a good example of constructional difficulties presented by the journey-out plot with its centrifugal emphasis. One of the prime reasons is that *Let It Come Down* emphasizes so sharply its social milieu, and the social world presents innumerable opportunities, and even demands, for clo-sure. The frequent marriage endings of many eighteenth- and nineteenth-century novels are emblematic of a deeply felt need for the novel, the most socially oriented of literary forms, to close with some kind of specifically social integration. That sort of in-tegration is much less common in the modern novel, where in-stead of the irregular being tamed, being brought within the *nomos* of society, what seems already relatively regular or inte-grated tends to slip out. This is the situation in Bowles' stories as well as his novels. In "Here to Learn" neither the marriage *nor* the return to the parental home provides effective closure. When social integration fails to take place, the inevitable result, in fic-tion, is that certain characters and their problems must be elimi-nated or otherwise left behind, as some of the most interesting ones are in *Let It Come Down*. This can be disconcerting, but it is altogether essential to the effect Bowles wishes to achieve.

What frequently disturbs readers of *Let It Come Down* is the dropping of Eunice Goode's poignant yet comical pursuit of Hadija when Dyar leaves Tangier in Thami's boat, and certainly,

if the novel is not to be seen merely as a schematic representation
of ideas, a kind of apologue, Dyar's movement outward and the
concomitant loss to the plot of Eunice and Hadija must work
dramatically as well as thematically. When I asked Bowles himself
about the dropping of Eunice, he replied that Eunice had "fulfilled her function" by the point at which Dyar leaves Tangier and
that keeping her in would have meant plotting "a different course
of action entirely." [10] Only by understanding how the novel's plot
works dramatically and what Eunice's function is can we understand why she must be left out of the book's last phase—and why
that omission is not an aesthetic fault. Dyar's drift into anomy
and away from any conception of self and purpose that could
save him is the central movement of *Let It Come Down*. Without
it, the rest of the novel would collapse into a series of loosely related vignettes. Essential to that drift is Dyar's relinquishment of
Hadija. He does not, *cannot*, love her. He is constitutionally in-
capable of weaving the social webs that foster a conception of
identity and provide at least a provisional sense of shelter for human beings. Moreover, he fails to understand the need for such
webs. He erroneously believes that identity can be found through
freedom, and freedom only through isolation. To be a "winner"
he thinks he has to escape links with others because he cannot
maintain those links without being dominated by them. It is
therefore necessary for Dyar to reject the social world and all its
possibilities for enclosure. Yet even as he half-formulates these
thoughts he tends to drift more blindly than deliberately away
from other people. His abandonment of Hadija seems casual,
but this is entirely in character. For Dyar to agonize over the decision, or even to regret it, would imply a degree of real emotional connectedness to her that simply does not exist.

But what of Eunice? Why does she occupy such a dominant
position in the novel's first half, only to be jettisoned in the second? The answer lies, as it always does in *Let It Come Down*,
with Nelson Dyar. Eunice must be fully realized and convincingly overpowering—a true threat to Dyar—for the reader to be
drawn into his pursuit of Hadija. Because Dyar's attachment to
the girl is so self-evidently shallow, the reader's interest can be
engaged in no other way. The full force of his abandonment must
be rendered, but it cannot be through Dyar's emotional makeup,

or even through his own point of view. The value of what he gives up must be represented through something external to Dyar, and that something is Eunice Goode, whose passion for Hadija is more intense than Dyar's and, in a curious way, less perverse. Eunice comes much closer to a strategy for survival than does Dyar. She has a conception of herself that keeps her afloat. But when she meets Hadija she realizes that what she has is not enough: "She was suddenly conscious of the world outside herself—not as merely a thing that was there and belonged to other people, but as something in which she almost felt she could share" (*LD* 58). This sad epiphany places Eunice light-years beyond Dyar in her understanding of the human condition and makes her a more suitable partner for Hadija, despite her possessiveness, than Dyar can ever be. The importance of Hadija lies not in the girl herself but in what she stands for: the possibility of being without being alone. Eunice realizes this and Dyar does not. The threat Eunice poses both fixes the reader's attention on the value of the prize (a human relationship) and partially obscures the fact that Dyar does not really love Hadija. By transferring to Eunice all the intensity and much of the significance of a relationship with Hadija, Bowles accomplishes the almost impossible trick of expanding the reader's appreciation of what Dyar is giving up without ever minimizing Dyar's own detachment.

Not only Eunice and Hadija, but the whole rich social fabric of Tangier is put aside when Dyar strikes out for the Spanish Zone, and other opportunities for closure are sacrificed as a result. The greatest sacrifice, and the one most intimately joined to the novel's primary movement, is Thami's. Thami plans to use his newly acquired boat as a source of financial independence from his wealthy brothers, the Beidaouis. Hassan and Abdelmalek have virtually disowned him for his failure to behave in a manner deemed appropriate for a Moroccan Moslem of high birth. But there is more to his motivation than that. He clearly wants to design for himself a social world in which he will feel neither self-exiled nor cast off by his brothers. Yet he also wishes for them to be a part of his world. The long party scene at the Beidaoui Palace is not just a decorative set-piece. It is absolutely necessary to establish unequivocally what Thami will leave behind when he takes Dyar out of Tangier. Thami's appearance at the party, uninvited, to ask his brothers for money to buy the boat, suggests a lingering desire to be thought respectable by his brothers, and to be, at least peripherally, a part of their world. Both brothers consider his presence an outrage, and one of them attempts, unsuccessfully, to frighten him off by sending Eunice Goode over to talk to him. When he goes to the Spanish Zone with Dyar, Thami, like most of Bowles' explorers, intends to return. But the book's centrifugal momentum will not allow it. The Beidaouis, as well as Thami's wife and baby son, must be left behind. They, no less than Eunice Goode, have fulfilled their function.

It is not difficult to see that, as Bowles claims, "the entire book is constructed in order to lead to this impossible situation at the end."[11] As if to reinforce this point, an extended scene immediately preceding the final section places Dyar in bed with Daisy de Valverde. The escapade, induced by majoun, is ludicrous, but it has its serious side, for it is Dyar's last chance to form a connection with the society he is on the verge of leaving behind. The absurdity of the situation, with a tray of food spilled all over the bed and Thami waiting outside in the garden, is more than sufficient to indicate the impossibility of any social bond or closure for Dyar. Daisy has grown somewhat fond of Dyar, but the feeling is hardly reciprocated. If Dyar has left Hadija without regret, he all but flees from Daisy. The social world, however, will not be abandoned so easily. Although Daisy's appearance at the little hut in the Spanish Zone is ostensibly for the purpose of helping Dyar out of his considerable legal predicament (and to recover the stolen money), the visit has a deeper significance too. It is a reaching out of the social world in the very direction of Dyar's isolation—a last, almost desperate insistence on his inclusion. When Daisy leaves, that social world, now "alien" to Dyar, departs with her, and Dyar remains in "that world of up here, like something of his own invention" (LD 291). As the novel ends, all complex, enveloping social structures have been left behind; nothing remains but a dead Moroccan and Nelson Dyar, standing by himself in the rain.

Bowles does not always handle these problems in the same way. When a journey out concludes with a coming home, either literal or figurative, characters who have been dropped can be reincorporated into the plot without serious damage to the work's integrity. This kind of development, however, inevitably carries with it a much greater degree of closure than Bowles' narratives usually possess. His strategies must be more ingenious. In "Here to Learn" Bowles relies on the time-honored tricks of abandonment and death: Malika leaves Tim after he postpones his return to Tangier, Tony leaves Malika, Malika goes to America with Tex, Tex dies, Malika returns to Morocco, where she finds that her mother has died. This formula is simple and works well enough within the framework of a novella, but in the longer narratives characters are more numerous, more fully drawn, and less easily dispatched. In *Up Above the World* and *The Spider's House* Bowles focuses his attention on the alien milieu after the main characters' arrival, and in doing so manages to keep most of the, ancillary characters "in" without sacrificing the sense that the protagonists (the Slades, Soto, Amar, even Stenham) are drifting outward. In *The Sheltering Sky*, perhaps the purest journey out among Bowles' four novels, he employs solutions quite similar to those he uses in *Let It Come Down*. The Lyles, like the Beidaouis, Mme Jouvenan, Hadija, Eunice, and Wilcox, simply fall out of the plot after having "fulfilled their function"; but Tunner, who is more closely bound up with the Moresbys, still has a role to play. His reappearance late in the novel is nearly identical to Daisy's in *Let It Come Down*, in that both characters are temporarily reincorporated into the plot to dramatize the hint or promise (ultimately unkept by the novel) of safe return. But because of the centrifugal dynamics of each book, neither Tunner nor Daisy can be part of any final closure.

Human fictions, as Marianna Torgovnick observes, are typically torn between the impulse to create coherence and the impulse to mimic life's disorder. Indeed, tension between the need to pattern inchoate experience and the fear that no ultimate pattern exists may form the basis of all human system-making. What we have in Bowles, no less (though less obviously) than in Thomas Pynchon, is an artist who recognizes this opposition and gives it thematic prominence. Consider these remarks in a draft fragment of a letter in the Humanities Research Center: "The phenomenological world is a mystery. To me everything is a mystery; and the human consciousness is slightly less of one only in the degree to which it aspires to discover a system of 'meaning' which can make the overwhelming fact of the mystery bearable."[12] The search for that meaning—a temporary shelter to make the mystery, the world outside, bearable—is Bowles' subject. His plots are centripetal enough, or sufficiently closed, to convey meaning, but they are centrifugal enough to hint strongly of meaning's ineluctably contingent nature. They are attempts at enclosure that delicately admit of failure. They move eloquently toward silence, toward (but never quite to) articulation of the moment after human speech ends.

5. Story as Shelter

I

STORYTELLING ITSELF is one of the most important and pervasive forms of shelter from the world outside. Ursula LeGuin explains the protective function of narrative in a way that is particularly germane to Bowles' work: "Why are we huddling about the campfire? Why do we tell tales—why do we bear witness, true or false? . . . Is it because we are so organized as to take actions that prevent our dissolution into the surroundings?"[1] Dissolution into the surroundings—the world outside the window—is what Bowles' characters fear most, although they do not always fully comprehend the nature of their anxiety. LeGuin is clever to connect storytelling with the image of the campfire. Our remotest ancestors, sitting around such a fire, must have found reassurance in the fact of their safe return from the day's dangers. And reassurance is the primary source of the impulse to enclose experience in narrative. Peter Berger takes this subject up in a discussion of "the ordering gesture by which a mother reassures her anxious child." In telling a child the story that "everything" is all right, Berger argues, the mother assumes the role of high priestess. She is telling the child to trust in the orderliness of the universe. Berger maintains that this experience is "essential to the process of becoming a human person." But his argument goes still further:

> In the observable human propensity to order reality there is an intrinsic impulse to give cosmic scope to this order, an impulse that implies not only that human order in some way corresponds to an order that transcends it, but that this transcendent order is of such a character that man can trust himself and his destiny to it.[2]

In Bowles, however, the "propensity to order reality" has quite a different implication. Humanly fashioned structures are not cor-

respondent with cosmic order but are defenses against an intuited cosmic *dis*order. The need for reassurance is the same, but
the reassurance is tentative, provisional, and ultimately unreliable. Like many of his younger contemporaries, Bowles rejects
the notion of a reality that is transcendently generated, revealed
as an absolute, and imbued with meaning. The only feasible way
to live in the kind of world Bowles' fiction reflects, one in which
cosmic emptiness presses against the windows of every human
life, is to keep filling that world with humanly created form. Precisely because experience is not inherently encapsulate, it must
be continuously enclosed. Bowles' characters do this, as most human beings do, in many ways, none of which is more important
than their telling stories to and about themselves, creating and
recreating their own experience. They build conceptual houses,
orderly structures that shelter them (or at least seem to) from the
awful vacancy and thus protect them from dissolution. Storytelling is, as Barbara Hardy has pointed out, "a primary act of
mind" that is "transferred to art from life." Everyone, Hardy observes, continuously constructs an ever-evolving autobiography
composed of such narrative modes as fantasy, memory, real and
imagined dialogue, lies, gossip, and jokes:

> As we sleep we dream dreams from which we wake to remember,
> half-remember and almost remember, in forms that may be dislo-
> cated, dilapidated or deviant but are recognizably narrative. We be-
> gin the day by narrating to ourselves and probably to others our
> expectations, plans, desires, fantasies, and intentions. The action in
> which the day is passed coexists with a reverie composed of the nar-
> rative revision and rehearsals of past and future.[3]

This is similar to what Julian Jaynes calls "narratization," in
which "we are always seeing our vicarial selves as the main figures in the stories of our lives." Jaynes goes on to say that "new
situations are selectively perceived as part of this ongoing story.
. . . until the picture I have of myself in my life story determines
how I am to act and choose in novel situations as they arise."[4]
Hardy convincingly demonstrates that this sort of activity occurs
not only in life, where it originates, but in virtually all novels.
What Bowles does is to emphasize the protective nature of his
characters' stories; like architectural forms, those stories shut

out the experiential terrors of emptiness and incertitude and tame them by bringing them inside. These narrative shelters are constantly being abandoned, demolished, rebuilt, and added onto, but while they last they provide (unlike life) some sense of closure and control.

The intrinsically false nature of storytelling is touched on by Roy Pascal in a lengthy discussion of Kermode's *The Sense of an Ending*. Pascal reminds us that Kermode's argument "starts from Sartre's critique of the traditional form of the novel, the chief falsity of which lies for him in the narrator (personal or impersonal), who writes from the standpoint of the outcome of the events related, and who thereby profoundly distorts the nature of real experience." Pascal further states that for Sartre, "the formal structure of the novel, like that of historical narrative, falsifies the very essence of reality as we experience it, since it establishes connexion and coherence whereas in reality events, even psychological events, are random and inscrutable." [5] Kermode of course diverges from Sartre at this point, insisting, as Pascal acknowledges, that no understanding is possible without the invention of fictions. But if we hold both these points in mind, and if we extend Sartre's "formal structure of the novel" to include all forms of storytelling, we come very close to the significance of story in Bowles' work. Storytelling *is* necessary both to meaning-construction and to the construction of the self and the social world; yet it also falsifies reality in some basic way that we can intuit, even if storytelling itself is our sole means of apprehending (or hypothesizing) that reality. The only meaning in Bowles is that which is humanly created, but the very fact of its human creation, its failure to correspond with or derive from a cosmic structure of meaning, renders it a temporary kind of shelter at best.

What is temporary and inadequate in Bowles' fiction is nevertheless essential. The underlying importance of storytelling to Bowles' work can readily be seen in his own retelling of the story of his father's alleged attempt on his life. It is a tale twice told, first by his grandmother to him, then by him to the world. The experience itself does not exist for Bowles except through the already enclosed form of his grandmother's telling. But it is sufficiently horrific, and sufficiently "real" (although its reality can be approached only through the mediating structures of story), that it requires retelling, reframing. It must be brought into the controllable interior of articulation. This attempt to bring the outside world in can be taken as paradigmatic of the functioning of storytelling in Bowles' fiction. His characters constantly build and rebuild narrative shelters to make a strange, inchoate, incomprehensible world seem more familiar. The making of those stories is one of their primary strategies for survival.

II

The Spider's House is filled with such shelters. One of the most interesting complexes of them occurs in an episode involving Lee Burroughs. When the situation in Fez becomes extremely tense on the eve of the Aïd el Kebir, a major Moslem holiday, Lee, along with Stenham, Amar, and Amar's friend Mohammed, leaves the city to attend an observance of the festival in the mountains, where the Istiqlal will not interfere.[6] As Lee watches the dancers around the bonfire, she begins to weave a story: " 'It's quite a show,' she said to herself contentedly, and she became interested in the pattern of the dance" (*SH* 318). Her initial narrative (that "it's quite a show") not only *precedes* experience but *determines* it. She knows she is interested at least partially because she has told herself so. The story constitutes a narrative house in which she is safe because she is interested, rather than frightened; and as an interested spectator she becomes more nearly a part of the scene before her and not so much an outsider.

But this shelter, like all of them, is only temporary. The narrative Lee constructs to make herself a part of the festival breaks down, leaving her exposed and afraid once more. Already, however, a new, more elaborate story is forming in her mind, in spontaneous response to her feeling of exteriority:

> It was as though she were living her life ahead of time. . . . She had seen herself back in Fez in the horrible little Hôtel des Ambassades, separating her valises from those of Stenham, alone in a cab riding to the station (as if there were trains running now, she thought with a sudden wry grimace). She was in the train with the new issue of *Time* and a copy of the Paris *Herald* on her lap; she was on the Algeciras ferry watching the gray, lumpy mountains of the African

coast slowly fade into the distance; she was eating shrimps under
an awning in a waterfront café, being brushed against by the news-
boys passing among the tables; she was sitting with the Stuarts at
Horcher's in Madrid with the treasure of her Moroccan trip stored
away in he memory, a treasure which would seem the richer for
being kept hidden, with only a piquant detail divulged here and
there—just enough to suggest the solid mass beneath the surface. "I
have so many things to tell you, but I don't know where to begin."
(*SH* 318–319)

It is remarkable how many interiors are fabricated in this narrative. Lee is in Fez, in the Hôtel des Ambassades, in a cab, in the
train, on the ferry, under an awning, in a café, at Horcher's in
Madrid, and most importantly, a character "in her memory"—in
the story she will tell to the Stuarts. That story is itself the deepest and safest shelter. She has already fictionalized herself once—
by placing herself within the narrative structure of the whole
passage. In the embedded story (the one she will tell little by little
at Horcher's) she is further "inside"—a fictional Lee inside a
story told by another fictional Lee inside a story told by the
"real" Lee, who is an outsider at the Aïd el Kebir.

Yet the frighteningly external experience that occasioned the
building of this intricate narrative house is still there, and it is not
to be denied:

The insistent drums were an unwelcome reminder of the existence of
another world, wholly autonomous, with its own necessities and
patterns. The message they were beating out, over and over, was for
her; it was saying, not precisely that she did not exist but rather that
it did not matter whether she existed or not, that her presence was
of no consequence to the rest of the cosmos. It was a sensation that
suddenly paralyzed her with dread. There had never been any question of her "mattering"; it went without saying that she mattered,
because she was important to herself. But what was the part of her
to which she mattered? (*SH* 319)

What Lee fears is what many Bowles characters fear—the loss
of self, or "dissolution into the surroundings," as LeGuin puts
it. The other, autonomous world is not just the festival, or even
Morocco, but the whole world outside. The festival is a shelter
for its participants, and for them it does have "its own necessities
and patterns"; but for Lee it is only a manifestation of the cha-

otic, indifferent external. Again we are reminded that protective forms are only invented things that provide for a time a sense of interiority for their inventors.

John Stenham's storytelling, as I have noted earlier, frequently assumes the aspect of self-deception. He fancies that he is detached from much that goes on around him, and he constructs a philosophy to legitimize that belief. He tells himself that "a man must at all costs keep some part of himself outside and beyond life." To Stenham, Fez represents "everything in the world . . . subject to change" (*SH* 203). So he stands outside the passing fair and its vulnerable shelters, but in doing this, he merely creates a new shelter—the fiction that he or anyone can be truly detached. That fiction becomes an essential component of his self-definition, and an assured sense of selfhood is a kind of narrative shelter that no one can long survive without.

Stenham's love for traditional Moroccan culture is another fictional shelter. Anthropologists have long been cognizant of the importance of storytelling in the understanding of alien culture. We form imaginative models or hypotheses about the other to bring it closer to ourselves and thus make it more nearly intelligible.[7] Stenham's storytelling follows this pattern, with a notable difference: for him, the protective function of familiarization assumes priority over intellectual curiosity. At the festival he narrates himself into interest in much the same way as Lee, and for much the same reason: "Telling himself it was a beautiful song, he decided to stand still and let it work upon him whatever spell it could" (*SH* 334). His need to perform this narrative operation, however, is not something that Stenham readily acknowledges, for he thinks of himself, despite his detachment, as an expert on Moroccan life. In some ways he is more appreciative of Morocco than are Lee, Moss, and Kenzie, but both his understanding and his appreciation are based upon conceptions of Moroccan culture that he himself fashions: "To please him the Moslems had to tread a narrow path; no deviation was tolerated" (*SH* 217). When a Moroccan whom he conceives as "pure" *does* deviate, Stenham is disconcerted, almost unnerved. Just before the crucial meeting in the café, Stenham and Lee spot Amar rescuing a dragonfly from a pool of water, and Stenham says, "He could be a Sicilian or a Greek. . . . Moroccans just don't do things like that" (*SH* 251). Stenham retains the notion that Amar fits into *his* picture of traditional Morocco, even though the episode of the dragonfly indicates that he does not. Much later, when Lee tells Stenham she has given Amar money for a pistol and thinks to herself, "So there's your purity" (*SH* 349), he is completely disoriented, replying, "I don't think I understand, Lee. It's too complicated for me" (*SH* 350). What has happened is actually rather uncomplicated. Amar has taken the money because he is poor and it was offered to him. Stenham is perplexed, then angered, simply because his view of things—the story he has been telling himself and in which he has come to believe—has been violated by an unpredictable reality.

For a novelist, Stenham has wondrously little insight into the nature and value of storytelling. His obtuseness on this point becomes vividly apparent at Si Jaffar's house when his Moroccan hosts engage in some storytelling of their own. In the Prologue, as Stenham is being escorted back to his hotel by the guide procured by Si Jaffar, he reflects on "the fluttering and whispering that had gone on at one end of the room about an hour and a half earlier" (*SH* 4). He correctly surmises that the story Si Jaffar tells him is told to mask the family discussion. It is incomprehensible because it is incomplete, being abruptly broken off as soon as the discussion at the other end of the room is concluded. But some two hundred pages later the same incident is related in greater detail. Si Jaffar's diversionary story is only the first; after tea, others are told: "As usual, Stenham found it impossible to follow these stories; he understood the words, but he never got the point" (*SH* 221). Si Jaffar attempts to explain one of them, but to no avail. Stenham, "expecting some further clue which might connect all the parts," comprehends "absolutely nothing of the story" (*SH* 222). At this point the reader becomes aware that the story passing through Stenham's mind in the Prologue is itself incomplete. He edits out, at that time, the part that disconcerts him: the knowledge that his lack of understanding derives not only from the first story's incompletion, but from his own inability to enter fully into the shelter of Moroccan culture. More importantly, he fails to recognize that storytelling has a sheltering function of its own—an idea that does not escape Si Jaffar: "Some of our stories are very difficult. Even the people from

Rabat and Casablanca often must have them explained, because the stories are meant only for the people of Fez. But that's what gives them their perfume" (*SH* 222). In understanding what gives stories their perfume—their ability to exclude as well as include, to conceal as well as reveal—Si Jaffar exhibits a greater sensitivity to the nuances and to the fundamental sources of narrative than does the professional writer John Stenham.

But it is Amar, the illiterate boy, who is the novel's master storyteller. A potter by trade, a creator of enclosures, Amar is skilled at shaping fictions that make life comprehensible, believable, and finally bearable. He is a born liar. He lies (or "invents," as he would prefer to say) so routinely that when he tells what he believes to be the truth, it is either a slip or an evasive tactic to confuse his interlocutor. He adopts this strategy when questioned suspiciously by Mokhtar Benani, the older brother of one of his companions:

> He would offer no information except that explicitly demanded by Benani, and then he would confuse him by telling the truth. Nothing could be more upsetting, because one always judiciously mixed false statements in with the true, the game being to tell which were which. It was axiomatic that a certain percentage of what everyone said had to be disbelieved. (*SH* 105)

Much later in the novel Amar's thoughts follow a similar trajectory:

> The Nazarene gentleman had told him that the Istiqlal spread many lies. He knew that; everyone told lies. It was for the intelligent man to distinguish truth from lies, just as it was only the intelligent man who knew how to lie in a way that made it next to impossible for others to find his lies and identify them as such. (*SH* 359)

What marks both these reflections is their assumption that truth exists apart from fiction and that it can be apprehended, though it need not be communicated to others. Amar's most durable shelter is his belief in that truth—in the very correspondence between human and divine order that appears to be absent from Paul Bowles' world. He recognizes that storytelling has an essential protective function, but he does not go so far as to abandon his conception of a truth transcending human narration.

In an essay published several years after *The Spider's House,*
Bowles elaborates on the subtleties of this kind of discourse.
"Mustapha and His Friends" is a character sketch of a typical
North African city-dweller of an age that has largely passed away.
This representative figure, whom Bowles calls Mustapha, "will
almost never say what is in his mind. For, according to his de-
vious reasoning, if he were to utter his true thoughts, he would
be giving himself away, playing recklessly into your hands." Furthermore, "he assumes that you would naturally like to be as accomplished a liar as he, but simply haven't the virtuosity." [8] The
idea, Bowles has told me, is "never to tell the truth but to mix in
some truth so that truth and non-truth become indistinguishable." And although Bowles has more or less disavowed the entire essay, omitting it from a recent reissue of *Their Heads Are
Green and Their Hands Are Blue* and assuring me that "the way
Moroccans communicate and relate to each other today is entirely different," [9] the piece does elucidate Amar's method of discourse and the philosophy that underlies it. Mustapha and his
friends, like Amar, spin fictions to protect themselves, but they
also believe in the existence of an absolute, determinate truth,
and this belief is the most effective protection of all.

Amar's storytelling is not simply a device to conceal his "true"
thoughts (although it does frequently serve that purpose). His
stories are woven into the fabric of his daily life to such an extent
that he is not always fully aware of the narration taking place. But
in each case, the story that is spun becomes a kind of shelter.
Often he reflects that his life is charmed, under Allah's special
protection:

> A great thing in Amar's life was that he had a secret. It was a secret
> that did not even have to be kept secret, because no one could ever
> have guessed it. But he knew it and lived by it. The secret was that
> he was not like anybody else; he had powers that no one else pos-
> sessed. Being certain of that was like having a treasure hidden some-
> where out of the world's sight, and it meant much more than merely
> having the *baraka.* Many Chorfa [10] had that. . . . But it was not this
> he meant when he told himself he was different from everybody
> else. . . . He had discovered that a hundred times a day things came
> into his head that never seemed to come into anyone else's head, but
> he had also learned that if he wanted to tell people about them—

which he certainly did—he must do it in a way that would make them laugh, otherwise they became suspicious of him. Still, if one day in his enthusiasm he forgot and cried: "Look at the Djebel Zalagh! The Sultan has a cloud on his shoulder!" and his friends answered: "You're crazy!" he did not mind. (*SH* 19–20)

The "truth" behind this characterization is his family's alleged descent from the Prophet, but Amar's narrative embroidery makes him special even within this tradition. The nature of his "powers" is interesting to note. The example he gives is nothing more or less than the creation of a metaphor—the germ of a story.

Many of Amar's narratives are highly colored by his dreams of Islamic glory—dreams that have their source in his sense of belonging to traditional Moroccan society. During a beating by his father, he constructs a story in which he becomes a revolutionary hero:

He was running down the Boulevard Poëymirau in the Ville Nouvelle with a sword in his hand. As he passed each shop the plate glass of the show window shattered of its own accord. The French women screamed; the men stood paralyzed. Here and there he struck at a man, severing his head, and a fountain of bright blood shot up out of the truncated neck. A hot wave of fierce delight surged through him. Suddenly he realized that all the women were naked. With dexterous upward thrusts of his blade he opened their bodies; with downward thrusts he removed their breasts. Not one must be left intact. (*SH* 25)

The story not only takes Amar's mind off what is really happening, but it also, like Lee's internal narrative at the festival, takes him away, making him a character within a setting that he himself shapes and controls. In this case pain is made endurable by transforming it imaginatively into the infliction of pain on others. Amar's fantasy protects him from his father's blows, and, by transferring his resentment to the French, it protects his father as well.

Throughout the novel Amar tells stories that grow out of his conception of himself as a defender of the house of Islam. At night he peers into the sky looking for light shining up "from the sacred shrine" (*SH* 33) in Mecca—a vision that originates in pictures on the walls of barbershops. From postcards he conjures up images of the holy Moroccan city of Moulay Idriss. He imagines the French being driven out "gloriously, with thousands of men on horseback flashing their swords and calling upon Allah to aid them in their holy mission as they rode down the Boulevard Moulay Youssef toward the Ville Nouvelle" (*SH* 49–50). When his companions dream "of Cairo, with its autonomous government, its army, its newspapers, and its cinema," Amar dreams "just a little beyond Cairo, across the Bhar el Hamar to Mecca," seeing "skies of flame, the wings of avenging angels, and total destruction" (*SH* 104). And always, each day of the eventful summer during which the novel takes place, Amar is perplexed by the discontinuity between the world that he imagines and the world that impinges itself upon his senses. This is why he must continue to invent, even as his frustration with the discontinuity increases.

Eventually Amar's storytelling begins to display a flexibility that derives from this frustration. His early, romantic visions are chiefly substitute realities, attempts to shut out the unacceptable. Later, when he meets Stenham, his storytelling begins to incorporate more of the threatening exterior. The protective purpose remains, but the enterprise has become more ambitious: to bring inside the structure of his stories that which is most frighteningly external. His first meeting with Stenham, and the construction he places on it, constitutes a turning point in his imaginative development:

> Now that he reviewed the events of the past two or three hours, it seemed to him that at the first moment when the man had come into the café he remembered having noticed a strange light around his head. A second later he had seen that it was only the glint in his blond hair. But now that their two fates were indissolubly linked, he recalled the brightness that had moved in the air where the man's head was, and preferred to interpret it as a sign given him by Allah to indicate the course he must follow. . . . From the moment he had seen the man's grave face . . . he had known that he could, if he wanted, count on his protection. It was even possible that in addition he might be able to add enough to his savings to buy a pair of shoes. (*SH* 267–268)

The conflict between the empirical ("the glint in his blond hair") and the imaginative ("a sign given him by Allah") can easily be seen in this passage, with the imaginative winning out. The idea of shelter is present, too, with the close association of religion, the protection of Stenham, and further financial security. But most significantly of all, Amar brings Stenham, a man so alien he is not even French, into his developing narrative. From this point on, the story of Amar and Stenham continues to expand in the boy's imagination.

Very late in the novel, when the old city of Fez has been closed by the French and Amar finds himself outside the walls, he goes to the house of resistance leader Moulay Ali, where he is encouraged to entertain guests by playing a *lirah:*

> Thinking of nothing, he played on, and slowly the person for whom he played ceased being the figure by the door, became that other presence he had become aware of . . . someone whose existence meant the possibility of hope. He stopped for an instant, and in his head, indissolubly a part of that happiness liberated by idea of the other being, he heard a second music—like singing coming from a far-off sunlit shore, infinitely lovely and inexpressibly tender, a filament of song so tenuous that it might be only the mind remembering a music it had never heard save in dreams. (*SH* 393–394)

In passages like this one, subtly but almost unbearably personal, the psychic sources of Bowles' creativity emerge with the strange clarity of those distant dreams. Readers always remark on similarities between Bowles and Stenham, but few notice how completely Bowles is Amar. What Amar evokes here is protection through a vision of primal well-being and repose—a safe place, indescribably remote and fragile. His sunlit shore is, on a level deeper than the fiction of *The Spider's House,* a fictional refuge from the snowstorm outside a window in New York in 1911.

"That other presence" is Stenham, whom Amar simply calls "the Nazarene." By this time Amar has been swept outside most of his accustomed shelters. He is separated from his father's house, from the walled city of Fez, and even from Stenham. As he plays his *lirah,* the house in which he sits is about to be ransacked by the French. He shortly makes his way onto the roof and is once more outside. When at last he finds Stenham again, he tries to reconstruct his recent adventures in such a way that external fact will merge with internal fiction, and Stenham will enter: "Then Amar told him his story. The man listened, but he seemed restless and distraught, and twice he looked at his watch" (*SH* 402). At the end of the story Amar thanks Allah and declares that he is "happy," perhaps in an attempt to authenticate the feeling engendered during his earlier reverie. But the effort is futile. Stenham remains aloof, his mind already preoccupied with his impending flight to Casablanca with Lee. There is no longer any room for Amar in his narratives. All that is left to Amar is his inventiveness. The fact that he has fashioned a myth of salvation involving an infidel is a poignant reminder that many of his shelters have crumbled, but it is also a testament to the imagination's elasticity and regenerative power.

III

That power is evident even when the mental faculty is impaired either through illness or drug use. The mind continues to spin out stories, and the underlying purpose of the storytelling is still to render experience at least partially intelligible. Two of Bowles' stories set in the United States, "You Are Not I" and "If I Should Open My Mouth," feature characters who are mentally deranged, and although neither character has what a rational person would call a firm grip on the experiential world, both keep afloat, more or less, by telling stories. The stories they tell, no less than those of "sane" people, give structure to their reality and make it bearable. "You Are Not I" is a first-person account of a woman's brief escape from a mental institution and her subsequent return. The narrator, called only "Ethel" in the story, walks away from "the Home" during the confusion following a train wreck. Winding her way through the survivors and the dead, she begins to tell stories within her story. Thinking resentfully about the freedom of movement enjoyed by the train's passengers, she conceives that someone in authority has given them (and, of course, not her) permission to travel. She quickly adds, however, "I know there is no chief who says things like that to people. But it makes it pleasanter for me when I imagine such a person does exist" (*CS* 157). She tells herself these stories—including the whole narrative that is also Bowles' story—for just this reason. She needs to make "it" (her life, her world) pleasanter. Paradoxically, it is the telling of stories, her only defense against complete mental chaos, that marks her as insane from the point of view of others.

If she is insane, she is clever as well. When a man catches her placing a stone in the mouth of one of the victims of the wreck and asks, "Are you crazy?" (*CS* 158), she replies that the woman on the ground is her sister, knowing that the statement is untrue. She consciously constructs a fiction that may prevent, or at least delay, her return to the Home. The ploy works; the man believes her to be one of the passengers on the train, and eventually she is delivered to her actual sister, who lives nearby. When she arrives at her sister's house, Ethel looks around and notices that everything is backward:

> She had even switched the stairs and fireplace around into each other's place. The furniture was the same, but each piece had been put into the position exactly opposite to the way it had been before. . . . I kept my mouth shut, but I could not help looking around with a great deal of curiosity to see if she had carried out the reversal in every detail. (*CS* 160)

Readers have to do some storytelling of their own here to sort out what is "really" happening from Ethel's account. When Ethel begins to laugh at the house's backwardness and her sister stares at her in undisguised fear, it becomes apparent that the house is backward only in Ethel's imagination. Her sister now understands that Ethel is still quite on the other side of the looking glass and decides to contact the Home immediately. A telephone call confirms that Ethel has escaped, and two men are sent to retrieve her.

But Ethel has other plans. Through the use of her "great will power" (*CS* 161) she intends nothing less than to alter reality. When the men arrive she at first resists, stuffing a stone into her sister's mouth until her lips bleed. This is the first stage of a much more comprehensive reversal than the one before: "Next, the two men had hold of my arms very tight and I was looking around the room at the walls. I felt that my front teeth were broken. I could taste blood on my lips" (*CS* 163). Again the

reader has to do some reconstruction, but the task is not difficult. Ethel tastes blood because she has stuffed the stone into her
own mouth, thinking that she is her sister; by trading places with
her sister she can stay where she is. In the next two paragraphs
she describes her sister, not herself, being taken away to the
Home. She even includes details of the journey that she could not
know without being there. She is, in fact, there, but in her own
mind a transfer has occurred that allows her to be free. In the
final two paragraphs she places herself comfortably at home and
her sister "in the Home, writing all this down on paper" (*CS*
163) as she herself used to do. The convolution at this point is
almost Nabokovian in its complexity. Ethel is telling a story (the
entire story) in which she tells another story (the "will power"
reversal) in which her sister becomes the author of a story in
which Ethel is a character. But her sister has long been the
author/authority for this helpless, confused woman. Little has
changed except that, back in the Home, Ethel has woven another
narrative tapestry to protect her from full knowledge of her insanity. Her story is both a symptom of her malady and a shield
against it.

"If I Should Open My Mouth," a story in the form of a journal, is more obviously "written" than "You Are Not I," and its
narrator is more consciously bent on defining himself through
the account he keeps. He is, unlike Ethel, quite self-analytical,
even though the results of some of his analyses are somewhat sus-
pect. Also unlike her, he is able to take care of himself, but he is
certainly not integrated into the social world or capable of behav-
ing in a consistently rational manner. Much of the journal chronicles his plan to put boxes of poisoned chewing gum in New York
vending machines. In one entry he describes in detail the delivery
of the first twenty boxes. His later discovery that he still has all
the boxes in a jacket pocket astonishes and bewilders him because he has come to believe what he has imagined and written
down. Faced with evidence that the escapade never took place,
he can only conclude, "Everything is all wrong" (*CS* 258).

The reason the narrator gives for keeping a journal—to link
himself with some kind of cosmic totality beyond space and
time—is specious. His real reason is to keep everything from
going all wrong. Unhappy with his "unsatisfactory life" (*CS*

252), a phrase he uses twice, he develops a more acceptable conception of himself in his writing. At one point he reflects on "that other person, the ideal one that I ought to be" (*CS* 254), and his depiction of himself in the journal is an attempt to actualize his ideal. But scattered throughout the journal entries are oblique references that hint of a distinct bifurcation in his personality. He is a lonely, embittered man whose self-respect and identity grow out of the story he tells. In the story he is a significant figure. This is why it is so important for him to read about his "crime" in the press. It unnerves him to find nothing: "The police assuredly are playing some sort of game. There must have been at least fifteen deaths, and not a word about one of them has appeared" (*CS* 256). His anxiety derives from a deep-seated need to read *another* story about himself—not just the one he is writing—to corroborate and bolster the image he has created.

During the days of waiting for a newspaper account to appear, the narrator is haunted by "a dream-vestige" which he cannot bring into focus but which is "connected with languor, forgetfulness, lostness, emptiness, endlessness" (*CS* 256–257). The dream crystallizes in his mind only after the discovery of the chewing gum boxes in his pocket. He describes it in his last entry in terms that make clear the true purpose of his storytelling:

> It is almost impossible to put down, since nothing *happens* in it: I am left only with vague impressions of being solitary in the park of some vast city. Solitary in the sense that although life is going on all around me, the cords that could connect me in any way with the life have been severed, so that I am as alone as if I were a spirit returned from the dead. (*CS* 258)

He goes on to say that "there are streets full of people" but he "will never be able to touch them." His sense of isolation is as intense as Nelson Dyar's at the end of *Let It Come Down,* and its source is much the same. He feels as if he does not exist, "for in order to *be,* one must not only be to one's self: it is absolutely imperative that one be for others. One must have a way of basing one's being on the certainty that others know one is there" (*CS* 258). The narrator conceives his poisoning plan, persuades himself that he has gone through with it, and looks for recognition of his deed in the newspapers all for the sake of being and making others know he is there. Loss of the social webs that contribute to the shaping of human identity can lead to the loss of identity itself. The narrator's journal is a means by which he repeatedly defines and redefines his own image, but that definition is meaningless, as he finally comes to understand, unless his story is "read" by someone else. At the end of this final entry he declares his intention of abandoning the poisoning scheme—but only partially. He will, he says, throw the contaminated boxes on the rubbish heap behind the school where "the kids" may find them. This ending, emphasizing as it does the narrator's continued isolation, points up again the close connection between what Peter Berger calls anomy and insanity. Any *nomos* we construct can easily fall apart. If human identity, the most basic and necessary *nomos* of all, is socially shaped, it cannot remain stable in the absence of social ties.

The use of drugs by many of Bowles' characters frequently influences the kinds of stories they tell, and, more often than not, drugs thwart the mind's ability to tell coherent, orderly stories that "enclose" experience and make it intelligible. Although Bowles, in his own blurb from *A Hundred Camels in the Courtyard,* calls kif "the means to attaining a state of communication" with others and with the self, Lawrence Stewart points out that kif and similar substances can have quite negative effects in Bowles.[11] In *Let It Come Down* the stories Dyar tells himself after eating Daisy's majoun and smoking Thami's kif increasingly propel him on a course of action that leads to his complete isolation. That process is already well under way, but the drugs certainly accelerate it. In *Up Above the World,* when Taylor and Day Slade are given morphine and scopolomine without their knowledge, the results are just as damaging. Day, under the influence of these drugs, finds herself able to construct a narrative, but it is one that does not adequately interpret or domesticate her experience: "Even while she was balancing at the edge of the abyss, she found herself wondering that it was possible to be in so decentralized a state and yet be aware, not only of everything inside and outside herself, but also of the fact that the disintegration was still in progress" (*UW* 119). Not long afterward, Day concludes that she is in a hospital, but since she can "remember nothing" (*UW* 132), the story she tells herself encloses nothing.

Because memory is the mental faculty essential for encapsulating experience, Day's conclusion—her narrative—is meaningless. This is of course Grove Soto's intention. If no understanding is possible without the invention of fictions, the most efficient way to sabotage understanding is to sever all connection between the mind's narratives and the experiences they attempt to structure.

All four of the stories in *A Hundred Camels in the Courtyard* (*CS* 295–306) have to do with the use of kif. One of them, "He of the Assembly," also exposes as starkly as anything in Bowles' canon the importance of storytelling in the construction of meaning. The story's main character is based on an actual Marrakech eccentric (or perhaps lunatic) named Boujemaa, which means "He of the Assembly." Boujemaa spoke in apparently unconnected, senseless fragments. Bowles' account of the story's genesis, as related by Lawrence Stewart, concisely defines the power of narrative to enclose: "By giving me these fragmentary sentences he aroused my curiosity to such a point that I had to explain it for myself by writing a story about it. It's explained to my satisfaction—my own, that's all. It's a story" (*PB* 129). The story seizes upon an elusive aspect of reality and interprets it, imposing on ragged experience the structure of articulation. "He of the Assembly" is a particularly interesting example of this process because its thematic focus is so clearly the process itself. The story is about storytelling—both the kind that satisfactorily orders experience and the kind that seems to distort it.

The most obvious structural division of "He of the Assembly" is the alternation between the title character's point of view and that of Ben Tajah, an older man. But more important to the story's meaning is the alternation between narration of outward events and the two characters' reflections on those events. He of the Assembly's reflections are largely kif-induced fantasies, the stories told by a distorted mind. Ben Tajah's tend to be explanatory stories he tells himself in an effort to interpret enigmatic experience. The chief enigma is a note Ben Tajah has found. The envelope bears his name, and the message reads, "The sky trembles and the earth is afraid, and the two eyes are not brothers" (*CS* 313). Ben Tajah reads the note while sitting in the Café of the Two Bridges in Marrakech. Shortly afterward the focus shifts to He of the Assembly, who is in the same café smoking kif.

The relationship that develops between the boy and the man constitutes much of the story's plot.

As He of the Assembly draws on his kif pipe, he begins to weave a story. The story seems superficially similar to the one Lee Burroughs tells herself at the festival in *The Spider's House*. Both take their creators temporarily away from their surroundings to another place. But there are two major differences. Lee's story puts her in a safer, more familiar place, while the boy's takes him out of the safety of the café and into the street, where he is in danger of detention by the police. Moreover, Lee's story serves its purpose and is gone, whereas the boy's fantasy continues to haunt him and to undermine his ability to interpret reality. The fantasy begins conditionally, as if to suggest his initial awareness of its fictiveness: "If I got up and ran down the street . . . a policeman would follow me and call to me to stop" (CS 313). But it quickly moves into the indicative mood as He of the Assembly surrenders to his story, letting it replace rather than interpret the world around him. He sees himself first pursued by the police, then rescued by an old woman who urges him to climb down a rope ladder into her soup-kettle, where a rowboat miraculously awaits him. As he boards the boat he looks up and sees the police capture the old woman. He rows the boat and ponders the fate of the woman. Suddenly he thinks of the café, and without transition he is back in it smoking his kif and noticing Ben Tajah.

Part Two of the story is exclusively concerned with Ben Tajah's attempt to understand the meaning of the mysterious note. He tells himself three interpretive stories, although none of them really satisfies him. When he discovers the letter missing, he concludes that someone has taken it, but he quickly discards that possibility, preferring to believe that there never was a letter. He thinks of going back to the café and asking the *qahouaji* (teamaker) if he saw him looking at the piece of paper, but he is afraid. If the *qahouaji* says no, the words were put into Ben Tajah's head directly by Satan, which would be far worse. This third explanatory story is the most unsettling one, and in any case, Ben Tajah is no closer to knowing what the message means or why he was chosen to receive it.

In the next two sections the focus is once again on He of the

Assembly, who continues to be confused by his recurring story of
the woman, the kettle, and the boat. Standing at a pissoir, he momentarily forgets where he is, again placing himself back in the
story "waiting for the rowboat to touch the landing pier" (*CS*
317). Even when he recalls that he is on a city street, his conception of the world is still shaped by the kif story: "Then he began
to walk very fast down the street toward the bazaars. He had just
remembered that the old woman was in the police station" (*CS*
317). The fourth segment is placed at the very center of "He of
the Assembly" for good reason. It is the boy's interior monologue, and much of it is related to his "real" experience in a dis-
jointed and peripheral way. There are some recognizable elements in it. He of the Assembly decides, for instance, that the old
woman who helped him is in "fact" a kind of witch, Aïcha Qandicha,[12] who is conspiring against him. Paranoid delusion is a
common feature of drug-induced storytelling in Bowles. On the
whole, the boy's impressions in the monologue are incoherent
and, to readers attempting to construct their own story of what
is happening, almost unintelligible. Nevertheless, these seemingly random reflections do constitute, like all storytelling, an
effort to shape experience, and they do undoubtedly make some
kind of sense to the boy, even though their logic is more the logic
of dream than of rational thought.

The last three sections bring Ben Tajah and He of the Assembly
together. Both characters have something to gain from the relationship. He of the Assembly feels safe from the police while
with Ben Tajah, and Ben Tajah feels safe from Satan while with
the boy. Ben Tajah is still evolving a protective narrative that will
make the letter comprehensible to him, and, increasingly, he in-
corporates the boy into the story. Perhaps, he ponders, He of the
Assembly has been sent to him to explain the message. Near the
end Ben Tajah and the boy sit quietly in the café and discuss the
note. Ben Tajah finally asks, "Did you ever hear those words?
Where did they come from?" He of the Assembly replies, "Yes,
I've heard them. But will you tell me what happened to me and
how I got out of the soup-kettle if I tell you about those words?"
(*CS* 323). Ben Tajah is desperately seeking an explanation—a
story that will bring the paper's strange message into the familiar
territory of human comprehension. He of the Assembly remains

unable to distinguish between his story and his experience apart from it. For Ben Tajah, narrative is a means to understanding; the mystery lies outside. For He of the Assembly there is no clear demarcation between the unfathomable world outside and the orderly world of human articulation. Both forms of storytelling have as their objective the structuring of experience. They differ primarily in terms of their effectiveness.

When the two promise to grant each other's wishes, they both lie. Neither has the knowledge that the other seeks. Their mutual assurances to the contrary are stories told to nurture and prolong their relationship. Ben Tajah is alone and afraid. He of the Assembly lives with his aunt but spends most of his time in the street, another of Bowles' many vulnerable, exposed young people. He and Ben Tajah need each other, and for a few very significant moments they manage to form (through their lies) a protective bond. The boy's explanation of the words on the paper is another lie. He tells Ben Tajah that the words are part of a song occasionally played on the radio. This falsehood, which leads Ben Tajah to believe that there never was a letter, is reminiscent of Marlow's lie to Kurtz's Intended at the end of *Heart of Darkness,* both in its utter untruth and in its utter necessity. Ben Tajah, having at last been told a story that makes his recent experiences comprehensible and acceptable, falls asleep. He of the Assembly, angered at Ben Tajah's failure to keep his part of the bargain, steals the older man's money. Folded in with the banknotes he finds the envelope with Ben Tajah's name on it. Inside is the cryptic message. In a final gesture of generosity, He of the Assembly burns the letter, and that burning is the coda to the story he has told Ben Tajah. The story is complete now, and Ben Tajah can rest peacefully, secure in his knowledge of the truth-as-told. But the letter exists, whether Ben Tajah knows it or not, and through it Bowles' story lays bare what the boy's story conceals: the existence of a reality that remains beyond the reach of storytelling, inchoate and inexplicable.

"The Hyena," a very short story with no human characters, displays with admirable efficiency both the uses and the limitations of storytelling. A stork, flying north over the desert, stops for water at a pool, where he meets a hyena. Although he has never seen a hyena before, he has heard that they are dangerous and have magical powers. After a lengthy debate with the hyena on this subject, the stork attempts to fly away but breaks his wing against a nearby cliff. The hyena invites him to his home, then tears his neck open, and ten days later eats the rotting corpse. This brief parable bears some obvious resemblances to Bowles' other works, and especially to "The Delicate Prey." The mainspring of both tales is a journey into unknown, potentially hazardous territory and an encounter with a representative of the intransigently alien. And in both stories narrative shelters protect the main characters until the inevitable moment when words fail.

The protective story that Driss and his uncles tell themselves at the outset of their journey guards them from fear of the Reguibat. It has been a long time since the Reguibat have attacked a caravan; they have lost most of their arms and ammunition; they have lost their spirit. It is crucial that the Filala believe these stories whether or not they are true; otherwise, they might never summon the courage to leave home. Later, when they meet the stranger in the desert, they tell themselves that he is safe because he comes from Moungar, a holy place. This time, however, their belief in the truth of a fiction is their undoing. Both stories make reality seem safer and more orderly than it is. "The Hyena" follows a similar pattern, except that the first protective story is replaced, not just succeeded, by the second. The stork has heard "that if the hyena can put a little of his urine on someone, that one will have to walk after the hyena to whatever place the hyena wants him to go" (*CS* 291). Armed with this knowledge, the stork keeps his distance. The hyena, reading the stork's mind, challenges him: "You think I have that power? Perhaps long ago hyenas were like that. But now they are the same as everyone else" (*CS* 291). The stork, now in the air again, remains skeptical, reminding the hyena that magic "is against the will of Allah" (*CS* 292).

At this point the hyena tries a new and more successful tactic. Playing on the stork's own legendary reputation as a saint and a sage, the beast implies that the stork really knows nothing of holiness or wisdom, for if he did, he would understand "that magic is a grain of dust in the wind, and that Allah has power over everything" (*CS* 292). By encouraging the stork to submit to the ultimate shelter, the protection of Allah, the hyena undermines the stork's belief in the old superstition that has kept him at a safe remove from the beast. When the stork breaks his wing, he is prepared to accept the hyena's hospitality. But that hospitality, like Grove Soto's and like the Moungari's friendliness, is itself a fiction, as the stork soon learns. Belief in this second story, the story of the hyena's harmlessness, leads to the stork's destruction. His throat ripped apart, the stork tries to shape one more comforting narrative: "There is no power beyond the power of Allah" (CS 293). His bill merely opens in silence, and the story of Allah's protective power is not told. This untold story has its analogues in the Moungari's song, stopped by sand, at the end of "The Delicate Prey"; in the Professor's lonely, inarticulate howling at the end of "A Distant Episode"; and in Royer's vain attempt to complete the quotation from Gide at the end of "The Hours after Noon." In each case the conflict between outside and inside, experience and the ordering of experience, is won by the external; but also in each case, the effort to tame the outside world goes on, heroically, to the last possible minute.

The stork perishes because he allows his own protective stories to be replaced by those of another. The hyena's stories shelter himself alone, not the stork; they are designed to lure the stork into his hungry grasp. A similar pattern dominates the "Tea in the Sahara" episode of *The Sheltering Sky,* perhaps the most striking instance of storytelling in all of Bowles' canon. In that story three girls wish to have their tea in the desert. They seek their fortune in a town called M'Zab, where they meet and make love with a young man who gives each girl a silver piece and departs for his home in the Sahara. Months later the girls, all of whom are in love with this man, travel into the desert first by bus, then by caravan. When they reach the Sahara, they leave the caravan and walk from dune to dune until they find a suitable spot to make tea. Eventually they are found dead, their glasses filled with sand. Their story is unnerving to Port Moresby not only because of the terrible emptiness at its core but because the situation it describes so closely parallels Port's own. That situation is also the most frequently recurring one in Bowles: the journey, the reaching out (here foreshortened considerably) toward another person's sphere of familiarity; the ultimate defeat of ceremony, story, enclosure, by the world outside. But, as in the case of the stories told by the hyena, it is the context of the telling, not the content of the tale, that determines its protectiveness. Port hears the story from his Arab guide, Smaïl, and Marhnia, a prostitute, during his long nocturnal walk away from the safety of his hotel at the beginning of the novel. He is already confused, somewhat anxious, and "annoyed" (*SS* 36) by their conversations in Arabic. They speak in Arabic deliberately to exclude him, and they tell him the unsettling story for much the same reason. The purpose is to keep him off balance, disoriented. By increasing Port's sense of outsidedness, they increase their own sense of safety and control. Gaining this psychological advantage, they make Port a part of their territory.

The way in which "Tea in the Sahara" fits into the larger story of which it is a part—*The Sheltering Sky*—reveals how completely Bowles' fiction turns on the confrontation of the external world by the pattern-making human mind. The story told by Smaïl and Marhnia has at its heart the openness, the vacancy that Bowles' characters keep striving to fill. As a structure of words, it is already a domestication of that vacancy—an outside colonized by the imagination but still recognizable as outside. The story, moreover, is contained within another story—the account of Port's walk, which as we have seen is closed in a way that "Tea in the Sahara" is not. Port returns safely to his hotel. But the account of Port's walk, an apparent paradigm of the novel that ends with a comfortable sense of safety, is itself contained within a larger narrative that ends much more like the tale of tea in the Sahara. *The Sheltering Sky* is a story within a story within a story. Efforts to enclose seem in the structure of the novel to compete with a strong inclination to remain open. It is as if Port, by hearing Smaïl and Marhnia's story, hears also a forecast of the terrible open ending of his own story. It is also as if Paul Bowles, by writing the novel (and by living in Morocco), continues the attempt to have tea in the Sahara—to enclose that openness within the structure of narrative.

Storytelling in Bowles often assumes the aspect of magic, simultaneously banishing the existent world and creating out of airy nothing a new world that is more inhabitable. Bowles has long been fascinated with the role of sorcery in Moroccan life, but his interest in the metamorphosing powers of magic extends even further back, into his earliest childhood. The stories he told himself then, many of which he wrote down, were often tales of secret, magical places that no one else could enter. His father, in particular, was shut out. Once while visiting his father's relatives in upstate New York, Bowles invented a list of "stations on an imaginary railway." He then printed the names on slips of paper and deposited them "at what seemed to be the proper spot for each, along the paths in the woods." His father, hostile when he first discovered the signs, relented somewhat upon hearing that his son had named the edge of a dry creek "Notninrivo," thinking the word meant "Nothing in the river." Paul told him it did not mean that, and his father immediately became hostile again. Shortly afterward Bowles destroyed all the signs, including the ones for O'Virninton and Notninrivo (O'Virninton spelled backward), vowing that his father "must definitely never know" the real meaning of the mysterious word (WS 20–21). This is a long description of a childish game, but Bowles describes it in considerable detail himself, and it does demonstrate rather pointedly the purpose latent in his youthful storytelling: the magical replacement of an unfriendly world with a friendly one, and the exclusion from that self-created interior world of all that is perceived as dangerous or frightening.

Near the beginning of "The Frozen Fields," Bowles' most explicitly autobiographical fiction, the little boy Donald contemplates his grandparents' farm and in doing so performs an imaginative operation remarkably similar to Bowles' own childhood storytelling:

> The house was the nucleus of an enchanted world more real than the world that other people knew about. During the long green summers he had spent there with his mother and the members of her family he had discovered that world and explored it, and none of them had ever noticed that he was living in it. But his father's presence here would constitute a grave danger, because it was next to impossible to conceal anything from him, and once aware of the existence of the other world he would spare no pains to destroy it. Donald was not yet sure whether all the entrances were safely guarded or effectively camouflaged. (CS 262–263)

For Donald the "enchanted world" replaces the one "other people knew about," if only temporarily. The preservation of that magical realm depends upon keeping the magic secret, guarding the entrances, keeping the outside out. Throughout Bowles' work doors and windows function both literally and figuratively as interfaces between the outside world and fragile, humanly created interiors. Their very existence calls attention to the vulnerability of the structures, physical or conceptual, into which they open. When Donald's mother raises his bedroom window slightly, the room, like June's room in "How Many Midnights," grows sharply colder as the wind rushes in. But there is another, countervailing significance that clings to entrances in "The Frozen Fields." On the train Donald scratches "pictures with his fingernail in the ice that covered the lower part of the windowpane by his seat" (*CS* 261). His father, a fitting emissary from the external world, commands him to stop. That night Donald breathes on the frosty windowpane in his bedroom, creating a hole through which he can see "blackness outside" (*CS* 265). By the following evening, the shape has not yet completely disappeared: "The hole he had breathed in the ice on the windowpane had frozen over thickly again, but the round mark was still visible" (*CS* 275). This is perhaps the most important detail in "The Frozen Fields," because here the meaning of windows converges with the meaning of storytelling. Donald is an embryonic artist. His choice of a windowpane for a slate is, on a deeper level than his conscious mind fathoms, an act of defiance of the brute external. When he scratches his marks on the windowpanes he transforms them into texts, leaving signs of a human presence—order, design, articulation—at the frontier of chaos. Bowles' entire career as a writer and as an expatriate can be traced in these patterns. The marks will not last long, but while they do, they are the very definition of humanity and the means by which, for a time, the terrors of the world outside can be reduced to nothing more terrifying than the spaces between words.

Notes

PREFACE

1. Paul Bowles, interview with Daniel Halpern, *TriQuarterly* 33 (Spring 1975): 164–165. [Hereafter cited as Halpern interview.]

2. Paul Bowles, interview with Oliver Evans, *Mediterranean Review* 1, no. 2 (1971): 12. [Hereafter cited as Evans interview.]

3. Paul Bowles, "The Art of Fiction LXVII: Paul Bowles," with Jeffrey Bailey, *Paris Review* 81 (1981): 80. [Hereafter cited as Bailey interview.]

4. Wayne Pounds, *Paul Bowles: The Inner Geography*, pp. 1–3.

1. INTERIORS AND EXTERIORS (I)

1. Paul Bowles, *Without Stopping*, p. 10. [Hereafter cited in text as *WS*.]

2. Tzvetan Todorov, *The Poetics of Prose*, trans. Richard Howard, pp. 144, 166.

3. Paul Bowles, *Collected Stories, 1939–1976* p. 165. [Hereafter cited in text as *CS*.]

4. Bowles himself disputes that label, calling himself "basically" a realistic writer whose fictions are more often "stories of anguish" than of terror (personal interview, 8 June 1986).

5. Johannes Bertens, for instance, finds that "The Delicate Prey" is "unrewarding" because it focuses on destruction "simply for its own sake" (Johannes Willem Bertens, *The Fiction of Paul Bowles: The Soul Is the Weariest Part of the Body*, p. 191).

6. Lawrence D. Stewart, *Paul Bowles: The Illumination of North Africa*, pp. 38–48. [Hereafter cited in text as *PB*.] Stewart also makes the case for Norton's affair with Racky as a re-enactment of that earlier liaison with Charles.

7. Although Bowles has indicated to me (personal interview, 18 April 1984) that he does not regard Racky's name change as very important, I must agree with Stewart that the original name, coupled with the original title, does reveal something about the story's patterns of significance.

8. The phrase is Ralph Rader's, from an unpublished essay on "The Delicate Prey" as an action structure.

9. Bowles, personal interview, 18 April 1984. A close reading of the first three chapters of *Without Stopping* leaves little doubt as to the story's autobiographical elements. The farm setting, the family dynamics, and not least the tension between father and son all appear to be drawn directly from Paul Bowles' childhood.

10. Uncle Ivor is evidently a fictional version of Bowles' Uncle Guy. See *Without Stopping,* pp. 40–41.

11. Bowles, Bailey interview, p. 70.

12. Paul Bowles, *Midnight Mass,* p. 107. [Hereafter cited in text as *MM.*]

13. Bowles, Halpern interview, p. 167.

14. Wilhelm Worringer, *Abstraction and Empathy: A Contribution to the Psychology of Style,* trans. Michael Bullock, p. 15.

15. Philip Stevick, *The Chapter in Fiction: Theories of Narrative Division,* p. 10. [Hereafter cited in text as *CF.*]

16. Thomas Pynchon, *V.,* p. 71.

17. Bowles (personal interview, 18 April 1984) has expressed to me his dislike of Pynchon "among others," but he also acknowledged a "philosophical" similarity between himself and Pynchon.

18. Gaston Bachelard, *The Poetics of Space,* trans. Maria Jolas, p. 7. [Hereafter cited in text as *PS.*]

19. Paul Bowles, *Let It Come Down,* p. 228. [Hereafter cited in text as *LD.*]

20. Peter L. Berger, *The Sacred Canopy: Elements of a Sociological Theory of Religion,* pp. 19–23. [Hereafter cited in text as *SC.*]

21. Paul Bowles, "A Novel Fragment," *Library Chronicle of the University of Texas at Austin,* n.s. 30 (1985): 70. [Hereafter cited in text as *LC.*]

22. Paul Bowles, Works 7, Ams/draft fragment and notes with A revisions written in notebook, signed on cover [15 pp], n.d., Paul Bowles Collection, Harry Ransom Humanities Research Center, University of Texas, Austin. This line also may reflect problems between Paul and Jane Bowles early in their marriage. In *Without Stopping,* p. 223, Bowles writes, "She had finally told me that my 'view of life' depressed her so deeply that when she was with me, everything seemed hopeless. . . . (Much later she confided that she was frightened of being alone with me, particularly away from New York.)"

23. Bowles, personal interview, 18 April 1984.

24. Millicent Dillon, *A Little Original Sin: The Life and Work of Jane Bowles,* pp. 58–59.

25. Stewart, *Paul Bowles*, pp. 83–84, identifies the source of the quotation as Gide's *Amyntas* and provides Bowles' own loose translation: "The time that flows here has no hours. But everyone's lack of occupation is so perfect, that it doesn't seem empty. That one is not conscious at all of there being nothing."

2. INTERIORS AND EXTERIORS (II)

1. Paul Bowles, *The Spider's House*, p. 186. [Hereafter cited in text as *SH*.] It is noteworthy that this interpretation of Moroccan architecture is uttered by Stenham, whose own preoccupation with security becomes increasingly clear. A less biased observer might add a word about the role of climate in the evolution of an architectural style that does not include a large number of windows.

2. The exiled sultan, as Commander of the Faithful, was regarded as the custodian of the "house." See Douglas Porch, *The Conquest of Morocco*, p. 8.

3. Readers occasionally notice that Port Moresby is also a town in New Guinea (the capital of present-day Papua New Guinea, in fact). Bowles has told me (interview, 18 April 1984) that the naming was intentional but denies any significance other than that Port Moresby is a place he has always wanted to visit.

4. Paul Bowles, *The Sheltering Sky*, p. 162. [Hereafter cited in text as *SS*.]

5. Stewart, *Paul Bowles*, pp. 59–61, discusses the role of the Lyles, particularly concentrating on differences between early drafts (which made Eric explicitly homosexual) and the published novel.

6. Paul Bowles, *Up Above the World*, p. 21. [Hereafter cited in text as *UW*.]

7. Bowles has told me (interview, 18 April 1984) that he was thinking of the nursery rhyme when he gave the novel its title: "But what I had in mind were the words that come after: *so high,* which was a sixties thing."

8. Bowles, Evans interview, p. 11.

9. Tony Tanner, *City of Words: American Fiction, 1950–1970,* p. 19. Tanner argues that the American imagination is torn between "an abiding dream" of freedom and possibility and "an abiding . . . dread" of conditioning and control. His provocative discussion of freedom and form in American literature has considerable relevance to Bowles' work, although he mentions Bowles only in passing.

3. GOING OUTSIDE

1. Paul Bowles, *Their Heads Are Green and Their Hands Are Blue,* p. vii.

2. Graham Greene, *Journey without Maps,* pp. 180–181.

3. Graham Greene, "The Lost Childhood," in *Collected Essays,* p. 16.

4. I first used this term in an essay entitled "*King Solomon's Mines:* Imperialism and Narrative Structure," *Journal of Narrative Technique* 8, no. 2 (1978): 112–123. I should make it clear that I never intended for the word "romance" to be understood as necessarily distinct from "novel" in this context.

5. John G. Cawelti points out that formula stories "become collective cultural products because they successfully articulate a pattern of fantasy that is at least acceptable if not preferred by the cultural groups who enjoy them." They "affirm existing interests and attitudes." See *Adventure, Mystery, and Romance: Formula Stories as Art and Popular Culture,* pp. 34–35. Tzvetan Todorov has discussed the sameness of popular literary forms. Cawelti would maintain that it is precisely this conforming to generic rules (rather than violating them in the interesting ways that we expect from masterpieces) that makes formulaic writing an appropriate vehicle for the transmission of societal "interests and attitudes": individual genius, which even Todorov admits creates its own genre, does not get in the way of shared cultural wisdom, or what passes for wisdom. See Todorov, *The Poetics of Prose,* pp. 42–52.

6. Edward W. Said, *Orientalism,* pp. 108, 60.

7. Joseph Conrad, *Lord Jim,* p. 15. [Hereafter cited in text as *LJ.*]

8. Shlomith Rimmon-Kenan, *Narrative Fiction: Contemporary Poetics,* pp. 123–125. [Hereafter cited in text as *NF.*]

9. There are of course other perspectives from which one might examine the pattern of outward movement in Bowles. One of the most interesting is Quentin Anderson's. In *The Imperial Self* Anderson finds established in American culture since the early nineteenth century "an alternate mode of self-validation that openly proclaims its independence of the fostering and authenticating offices of the family and society" (pp. vii–viii). Anderson persuasively argues that "the American flight from culture, from the institutions and emotional dispositions of associated life, took on form in the work of Emerson" (p. 3). It is possible, up to a point, to see Bowles as an heir to this tradition. Like Anderson's imperial self, Bowles' characters try "to advance upon the flux of reality and make it their own" (p. 206), but not at all with the assurance of an Emerson, who confidently aspired, in Anderson's words, to "the power

to dispose of the whole created world as a woman arranges her skirt" (p. 56). And whereas attempts at domestication of the outside world in Bowles proceed from an intensely perceived sense of alienation (what I have called, and what Bowles himself calls, "outsidedness"), the imperial self does not accept the premise that the world has the power to exclude it. Alienation is not a possibility. Finally, the dichotomy between self and society is not nearly so distinct in Bowles as the one Anderson describes. Bowles characters often seek (however unsuccessfully) security and selfhood within the shelter of family, society, and culture.

10. Paul Bowles, Works 4, Notebook 4, n.d., Paul Bowles Collection, Harry Ransom Humanities Research Center, University of Texas, Austin. This is not the same unfinished novel as the one discussed earlier.

11. Bowles, personal interview, 18 April 1984.

12. As Paul Fussell explains it, "the explorer moves toward the risks of the formless and the unknown," while "the tourist moves toward the security of pure cliché," with the traveler mediating "between the two poles." See *Abroad: British Literary Traveling between the Wars,* pp. 38–39.

13. Paul Bowles, "A Talk with Paul Bowles," with Harvey Breit, *New York Times Book Review,* 9 March 1952, p. 19.

14. Bowles, Bailey interview, p. 92.

15. Bowles, personal interview, 8 June 1986. In this same conversation Bowles went on to explain that while the conversations are fictionalized, the basic material of the book is "all factual."

16. Paul Bowles, *Points in Time,* p. 18 [Hereafter cited in text as *PT.*]

17. Both Stewart (*Paul Bowles,* pp. 136–144) and Bertens (*The Fiction of Paul Bowles,* pp. 218–230) discuss this long story in detail.

18. Bowles, Bailey interview, p. 79.

4. THE SHAPES OF BOWLES' FICTION

1. Marianna Torgovnick, *Closure in the Novel,* p. 7.

2. John Kucich, "Action in the Dickens Ending: *Bleak House* and *Great Expectations,*" *Nineteenth-Century Fiction* 33, no. 1 (1978): 89. See also Frank Kermode, *The Sense of an Ending.*

3. Stevick, *The Chapter in Fiction,* p. 8. He is quoting from James' Preface to *Roderick Hudson.* See also Worringer, *Abstraction and Empathy,* p. 44.

4. Gérard Genette, *Narrative Discourse: An Essay in Method,* trans. Jane E. Lewin, p. 40. [Hereafter cited in text as *ND.*]

5. Bowles, Evans interview, p. 6.

6. Paul Bowles, Works 1, B [n.d.], Paul Bowles Collection, Harry Ransom Humanities Research Center, University of Texas, Austin. Bowles has stated, in an undated note to me (received June 1985), that "this concept and procedure no longer existed once I started to write the book."

7. Bowles, Evans interview, p. 6.

8. Robert M. Adams, *Strains of Discord: Studies in Literary Openness,* p. 13. See also Alan Friedman, *The Turn of the Novel.*

9. Bowles, Evans interview, p. 11.

10. Bowles, personal interview, 18 April 1984.

11. Bowles, Evans interview, p. 11.

12. Paul Bowles, AL/draft fragments to [unidentified recipient] *re* Christian element in his work, written in notebook signed on cover, n.d., Paul Bowles Collection, Harry Ransom Humanities Research Center, University of Texas, Austin.

5. STORY AS SHELTER

1. Ursula K. LeGuin, "It Was a Dark and Stormy Night; or, Why Are We Huddling about the Campfire?" in *On Narrative,* ed. W. J. T. Mitchell, p. 194.

2. Peter L. Berger, *A Rumor of Angels: Modern Society and the Rediscovery of the Supernatural,* p. 66.

3. Barbara Hardy, *Tellers and Listeners: The Narrative Imagination,* p. 4.

4. Julian Jaynes, *The Origin of Consciousness in the Breakdown of the Bicameral Mind,* pp. 63–64.

5. Roy Pascal, "Narrative Fictions: A Comment on Frank Kermode's *The Sense of an Ending," Novel* 11, no. 1 (1977): 40, 46.

6. By preventing observance of the festival in Fez (on the grounds that the true Sultan, whose participation was indispensable, had been exiled), the Istiqlal hoped to fan further flames of resentment against the French.

7. See especially Clifford Geertz, *The Interpretation of Cultures,* pp. 7–16.

8. Paul Bowles, *Their Heads Are Green and Their Hands Are Blue,* pp. 64–65.

9. Bowles, personal interview, 18 April 1984. The difference, Bowles explained, has to do with the way a subject people communicate with each other under a colonial master as opposed to the freer forms of discourse in which they can indulge after independence. Any astute tourist

in Morocco will observe, however, that many of the old techniques of discourse still prevail—at least in the presence of western visitors.

10. *Baraka* is a sort of special blessedness or grace thought to be conferred on some people in North Africa, particularly on the *Chorfa*, or descendants of Mohammed. See Clifford Geertz, *Islam Observed: Religious Developments in Morocco and Indonesia*, p. 44, for a succinct and lucid explanation of *baraka*.

11. Stewart, *Paul Bowles*, p. 119. Stewart also notes that Bowles himself has become "somewhat less enthusiastic" (127) in his admiration for kif since *A Hundred Camels in the Courtyard* was published in 1962.

12. Aïcha Qandicha, Bowles has explained (Evans interview, p. 94), is a vestige of pre-Islamic religious belief in Morocco: "Since she was still here in some force when Islam arrived, she had to be reckoned with. So she became this beautiful but dreaded spirit who still frequented running water and hunted men in order to ruin them."

Abbreviations Used

CF: Philip Stevick, *The Chapter in Fiction*
CS: Paul Bowles, *Collected Stories, 1939–1976*
LC: Paul Bowles, "A Novel Fragment," *Library Chronicle of the University of Texas at Austin* (1985)
LD: Paul Bowles, *Let It Come Down*
LJ: Joseph Conrad, *Lord Jim*
MM: Paul Bowles, *Midnight Mass*
ND: Gérard Genette, *Narrative Discourse*
NF: Shlomith Rimmon-Kenan, *Narrative Fiction*
PB: Lawrence D. Stewart, *Paul Bowles: The Illumination of North Africa*
PS: Gaston Bachelard, *The Poetics of Space*
PT: Paul Bowles, *Points in Time*
SC: Peter L. Berger, *The Sacred Canopy*
SH: Paul Bowles, *The Spider's House*
SS: Paul Bowles, *The Sheltering Sky*
UW: Paul Bowles, *Up Above the World*
WS: Paul Bowles, *Without Stopping*

Bibliography

Adams, Robert M. *Strains of Discord: Studies in Literary Openness.* Ithaca: Cornell University Press, 1958.

Anderson, Quentin. *The Imperial Self.* New York: Knopf, 1971.

Bachelard, Gaston. *The Poetics of Space.* Translated by Maria Jolas. Boston: Beacon Press, 1969.

Berger, Peter L. *A Rumor of Angels: Modern Society and the Rediscovery of the Supernatural.* Garden City, N.Y.: Doubleday, 1969.

———. *The Sacred Canopy: Elements of a Sociological Theory of Religion.* Garden City, N.Y.: Anchor Books, 1969.

Bertens, Johannes Willem. *The Fiction of Paul Bowles: The Soul Is the Weariest Part of the Body.* Amsterdam: *Costerus,* n.s. 21 (1979).

Bowles, Paul. AL/draft fragments to [unidentified recipient] *re* Christian element in his work, written in notebook signed on cover, n.d. Paul Bowles Collection. Harry Ransom Humanities Research Center, University of Texas, Austin.

———. "The Art of Fiction LXVII: Paul Bowles." With Jeffrey Bailey. *Paris Review* 81 (1981): 63–98.

———. *Collected Stories, 1939–1976.* Santa Barbara: Black Sparrow Press, 1981.

———. Interview with Oliver Evans. *Mediterranean Review* 1, no. 2 (1971): 3–15.

———. Interview with Daniel Halpern. *TriQuarterly* 33 (Spring 1975): 159–177.

———. *Let It Come Down.* Santa Barbara: Black Sparrow Press, 1980.

———. *Midnight Mass.* Santa Barbara: Black Sparrow Press, 1981.

———. *Next to Nothing: Collected Poems, 1926–1977.* Santa Barbara: Black Sparrow Press, 1981.

———. "A Novel Fragment." *Library Chronicle of the University of Texas at Austin,* n.s. 30 (1985): 67–71.

———. Personal interviews. 18 April 1984; 8 June 1986.

———. *Points in Time.* New York: Ecco Press, 1984.

———. *The Sheltering Sky.* New York: New Directions, 1964.

———. *The Spider's House.* Santa Barbara: Black Sparrow Press, 1982.

————. "A Talk with Paul Bowles." With Harvey Breit. *New York Times Book Review,* 9 March 1952, p. 19.

————. *Their Heads Are Green and Their Hands Are Blue.* New York: Random House, 1963. (Reprinted, New York: Ecco Press, 1984.)

————. *Up Above the World.* New York: Ecco Press, 1982.

————. *Without Stopping.* New York: G. P. Putnam's Sons, 1972. (Reprinted, New York: Ecco Press, 1985.)

————. Works 1, B [n.d.], Paul Bowles Collection. Harry Ransom Humanities Research Center, University of Texas, Austin.

————. Works 4, Notebook 4, n.d. Paul Bowles Collection. Harry Ransom Humanities Research Center, University of Texas, Austin.

————. Works 7, Ams/draft fragment and notes with A revisions written in notebook, signed on cover [15 pp], n.d. Paul Bowles Collection. Harry Ransom Humanities Research Center, University of Texas, Austin.

————. *Yallah.* With photographs by Peter W. Haerberlin. New York: McDowell, Obolensky, 1957.

Cawelti, John G. *Adventure, Mystery, and Romance: Formula Stories as Art and Popular Culture.* Chicago: University of Chicago Press, 1976.

Collins, Jack. "Approaching Paul Bowles." *Review of Contemporary Fiction* 2, no. 3 (1982): 55–63.

Conrad, Joseph. *Lord Jim.* New York: Houghton Mifflin, 1958.

Dillon, Millicent. *A Little Original Sin: The Life and Work of Jane Bowles.* New York: Holt, Rinehart and Winston, 1981.

Eisinger, Chester E. "Paul Bowles and the Passionate Pursuit of Disengagement." In Eisinger's *Fiction of the Forties,* pp. 283–288. Chicago: University of Chicago Press, 1963.

Emerson, Stephen. "Endings and *The Sheltering Sky.*" *Review of Contemporary Fiction* 2, no. 3 (1982): 73–75.

Evans, Oliver. "Paul Bowles and the 'Natural' Man." *Critique* 3 (1959): 43–59.

Friedman, Alan. *The Turn of the Novel.* New York: Oxford University Press, 1966.

Fussell, Paul. *Abroad: British Literary Traveling between the Wars.* New York: Oxford University Press, 1980.

Geertz, Clifford. *The Interpretation of Cultures.* New York: Basic Books, 1973.

————. *Islam Observed: Religious Developments in Morocco and Indonesia.* Chicago: University of Chicago Press, 1968.

Genette, Gérard. *Narrative Discourse: An Essay in Method.* Translated by Jane E. Lewin. Ithaca: Cornell University Press, 1983.

Greene, Graham. *Journey without Maps.* New York: Penguin, 1981.
———. "The Lost Childhood." In *Collected Essays,* pp. 13–19. New York: Viking, 1969.
Hardy, Barbara. *Tellers and Listeners: The Narrative Imagination.* London: Athlone Press, 1975.
Hassan, Ihab H. "The Pilgrim as Prey: A Note on Paul Bowles." *Western Review* 19 (1954): 23–36.
Hauptman, Robert. "Paul Bowles and the Perception of Evil." *Review of Contemporary Fiction* 2, no. 3 (1982): 71–73.
Jaynes, Julian. *The Origin of Consciousness in the Breakdown of the Bicameral Mind.* Boston: Houghton Mifflin, 1976.
Kermode, Frank. *The Sense of an Ending.* New York: Oxford University Press, 1967.
Kucich, John. "Action in the Dickens Ending: *Bleak House* and *Great Expectations.*" *Nineteenth Century Fiction* 33, no. 1 (1978): 88–109.
LeGuin, Ursula K. "It Was a Dark and Stormy Night: or, Why Are We Huddling about the Campfire?" In *On Narrative,* edited by W. J. T. Mitchell, pp. 187–195. Chicago: University of Chicago Press, 1981.
Lehan, Richard. "Existentialism in Recent American Fiction: The Demonic Quest." *Texas Studies in Literature and Language* 1 (1959): 181–202.
Lesser, Wendy. "Paul Bowles' *Collected Stories.*" *Review of Contemporary Fiction* 2, no. 3 (1982): 50–52.
Malin, Irving. "Drastic Points." *Review of Contemporary Fiction* 2, no. 3 (1982): 30–32.
Metcalf, Paul. "A Journey in Search of Bowles." *Review of Contemporary Fiction* 2, no. 3 (1982): 32–41.
Mottram, Eric. "Paul Bowles: Stacity and Terror." *Review of Contemporary Fiction* 2, no. 3 (1982): 6–30.
Pascal, Roy. "Narrative Fictions: A Comment on Frank Kermode's *The Sense of an Ending.*" *Novel* 11, no. 1 (1977): 40–50.
Patteson, Richard F. "The External World of Paul Bowles." *Perspectives on Contemporary Literature* (University Press of Kentucky) 10 (1984): 16–22.
———. "Paul Bowles: Two Unfinished Projects." *Library Chronicle of the University of Texas at Austin,* n.s. 30 (1985): 57–65.
Porch, Douglas. *The Conquest of Morocco.* New York: Knopf, 1983.
Pounds, Wayne. "*Let It Come Down* and Inner Geography." *Review of Contemporary Fiction* 2, no. 3 (1982): 42–50.
———. *Paul Bowles: The Inner Geography.* New York: Peter Lang, 1985.

———. "Paul Bowles and *The Delicate Prey:* The Psychology of Preda-
tion." *Revue Belge de Philologie et d'Histoire* 59, no. 3 (1981):
620–633.
Pynchon, Thomas. *V.* New York: Bantam, 1968.
Rimmon-Kenan, Shlomith. *Narrative Fiction: Contemporary Poetics.*
New York: Methuen, 1983.
Said, Edward W. *Orientalism.* New York: Vintage, 1979.
Stevick Philip. *The Chapter in Fiction: Theories of Narrative Division.*
Syracuse: Syracuse University Press, 1970.
Stewart, Lawrence D. *Paul Bowles: The Illumination of North Af-
rica.* Carbondale and Edwardsville: Southern Illinois University Press,
1974.
———. "Paul Bowles and 'The Frozen Fields' of Vision." *Review of
Contemporary Fiction* 2, no. 3 (1982): 64–71.
Tanner, Tony. *City of Words: American Fiction, 1950–1970.* New York:
Harper and Row, 1971.
Todorov, Tzvetan. *The Poetics of Prose.* Translated by Richard Howard.
Ithaca: Cornell University Press, 1980.
Torgovnick, Marianna. *Closure in the Novel.* Princeton: Princeton Uni-
versity Press, 1981.
Wells, Linda S. "Paul Bowles: 'Do not appropriate *my* object.'" *Review
of Contemporary Fiction* 2, no. 3 (1982): 75–84.
Worringer, Wilhelm. *Abstraction and Empathy: A Contribution to the
Psychology of Style.* Translated by Michael Bullock. New York: Inter-
national Universities Press, 1953.

Index

Adams, Robert M., 94
Aïcha Qandicha, 125, 139n.12
Aïd el Kebir, 86, 109–110
Anderson, Quentin, 136–137n.9

Bachelard, Gaston, 15–16, 22, 51, 59, 74
Baraka, 114, 139n.10
Baudelaire, Charles, 26
Berger, Peter, 18, 38, 56, 106, 122
Bertens, Johannes, xi–xii, 22, 133n.5
Bowles, Jane, ix, 25, 134n.22
Bowles, Paul: childhood of, 1, 2, 12, 54, 129–130, 134n.10; as "gothic" writer, 4, 133n.4; influences on, ix; marriage of, 25, 134n.22; travels and life abroad of, ix, 25, 54, 76, 82, 129
—works of: "At Paso Rojo," 66–68; "Call at Corazón," 24–26, 34; "The Circular Valley," 93; "The Delicate Prey," 4–6, 10, 18, 39, 64, 127, 128; "A Distant Episode," x, 17, 62–64, 70, 71, 128; "Doña Faustina," 8; "The Echo," 17, 19–20, 45, 66, 67; "The Frozen Fields," 8, 11–13, 14, 19, 45, 66, 130–131; "The Garden," 98–99; "He of the Assembly," 123–126; "Here to Learn," 17, 18, 71–74, 81, 83, 95, 100, 104; "The Hours after Noon," 26–30, 67, 128; "How Many Midnights," 3, 18, 20–22, 26, 34, 42, 47, 81, 95, 131; A Hundred Camels in the Courtyard, 122, 123; "The Hyena," 126–129; "If I Should Open My Mouth," 8, 44, 93, 118, 120–122; "In the Red Room," 17, 18; "Kitty," 8, 13–14; Let It Come Down, 16–17, 42, 47–53, 64, 67, 70, 79, 100–104, 121, 122; "A Man Must Not Be Very Moslem," 54; "Midnight Mass," 3; "Mustapha and His Friends," 75, 114; "Pages from Cold Point," xi, 8–11, 12, 41, 44, 66; "Pastor Dowe at Tacaté," 57, 60–62, 68, 71; Points in Time, 76–77, 137n.15; "Reminders of Bouselham," 7, 19; "Señor Ong and Señor Ha," 7; The Sheltering Sky, x, 6–7, 38–43, 44, 45, 46, 58, 68–70, 71, 77, 93, 95–98, 99, 104, 129; The Spider's House, ix, 3, 31–38, 54, 55, 78, 80–83, 85–92, 93, 99–100, 104, 109–118, 124; "Tapiama," 67, 70; "Tea on the Mountain," 78–80; Their

Heads Are Green and Their Hands Are Blue, 54, 75, 82, 114; "The Time of Friendship," 77–78; unpublished works, 22–24, 64–66, 67; *Up Above the World,* x, 3, 7, 17, 41, 42, 43–47, 66, 70, 92–95, 104, 122, 123; *Without Stopping,* ix, xiii, 1–3, 12, 45, 134nn.9, 10,22; "You Are Not I," 118–120; "You Have Left Your Lotus Pods on the Bus," 74–75
Breit, Harvey, 75
Burmese Days (Orwell), 80

Caesar, Irving, 62
Camus, Albert, 48
Casablanca, 31, 37, 81, 113, 118
Cawelti, John G., 136n.5
Chorfa, 114, 139n.10
Communist Party, 34–35
Conrad, Joseph, xiii, 15, 58–60, 66, 69, 126
Culler, Jonathan, 60

Darwin, Charles, 57
Dillon, Millicent, 25

Emerson, Ralph Waldo, 136n.9

Fez, 31, 33, 34, 35, 36, 55, 80, 87, 109, 110, 111, 113, 117, 138n.6
Filala, 4, 5, 127
Forster, E. M., 60, 81
Freud, Sigmund, xii
Fussell, Paul, 137n.12

Geertz, Clifford, 139n.10
Genette, Gérard, 90, 92
Gide, André, 27, 48, 128, 135n.25
Greene, Graham, 44, 54–55, 60

Haggard, H. Rider, xiii, 55, 62, 64, 66, 67
Hardy, Barbara, 107
Hashish, 4, 6, 17. *See also* Kif; Majoun
Heart of Darkness (Conrad), 66, 69, 126
Hemingway, Ernest, 25

Imperialist romance, 55–58, 60
Istiqlal, 32, 80, 82, 88, 109, 138n.6

James, Henry, ix, 2
Jaynes, Julian, 107

Karouine mosque, 37
Kermode, Frank, 84, 108
Kif, 50, 52, 53, 88, 122, 123, 124, 125, 139n.11. *See also* Hashish; Majoun
King Solomon's Mines (Haggard), 55, 64
Koran, 37, 79, 88
Kucich, John, 84

Laing, R. D., xii
LeGuin, Ursula, 106, 110
Lord Jim (Conrad), 58–60

Macbeth, 42, 94
Majoun, 50, 51, 52, 53, 103, 122. *See also* Hashish; Kif
Marrakech, 123
Matthiessen, Peter, 60
Mohammed V. *See* Sidi Mohammed
Morocco: history and culture of, 31–34, 36–38, 47, 76–77, 78–83, 86–88, 109, 114–117, 138–139n.9

Moulay Idriss, 116; shrine of, 37
Mrabet, Mohammed, ix

Naipaul, V. S., x, 60

O'Connor, Flannery, 7
Oran, 69, 96–97
Orwell, George, 60, 80

Pascal, Roy, 108
Passage to India, A (Forster), 81
Perry, Menakhem, 60
Poe, Edgar Allan, ix, xii
Polanski, Roman, 94
Port Moresby, New Guinea,
    135 n.3
Pounds, Wayne, xi–xii
Pynchon, Thomas, 15, 97, 104,
    134 n.17

Rabat, 113
Rader, Ralph, 134 n.8
Reguibat, 4–5, 127
Rimmon-Kenan, Shlomith, 60, 91
Robinson Crusoe (Defoe), 58

Sahara, 4, 38–39, 68, 77, 99,
    129

Said, Edward, 56
Sartre, Jean-Paul, 108
Schreiner, Olive, 58
Sidi Mohammed (Mohammed
    V), 31
Sri Lanka (Ceylon), 17, 18, 23,
    82
Stein, Gertrude, ix
Stevick, Philip, 15, 84–85, 95
Stewart, Lawrence D., xi–xii, 10,
    65, 122, 123, 133 n.6,
    135 nn.25,7, 139 n.11

Tafilalet, 4, 6
Tangier, ix, 26, 27, 47, 48, 50,
    52, 78, 101, 102
Tanner, Tony, 48, 135 n.9
Thousand and One Nights, The,
    38, 84, 87
Todorov, Tzvetan, 2, 3, 136 n.5
Torgovnick, Marianna, 84, 104

V. (Pynchon), 15, 97

Weil, Simone, 24
Wells, H. G., 58
Worringer, Wilhelm, 15, 84

Lightning Source UK Ltd.
Milton Keynes UK
UKHW010319230620
365308UK00017B/218